A GUIDE TO FORTRAN IV

A GUIDE TO FORTRAN IV

By SEYMOUR V. POLLACK

NEW YORK AND LONDON 1965
COLUMBIA UNIVERSITY PRESS 

Seymour V. Pollack is Associate Director of the Medical Computer Center, School of Medicine, University of Cincinnati, and coauthor, with Theodor D. Sterling, of Computers and the Life Sciences.

Printed in the United States of America

To

Sydell

Mark

Sherie

CONTENTS

A GUIDE TO FORTRAN IV

Chapter I

Basic Rules and Concepts

For those who have not previously worked with or read about computers it will be well to define some of the terms so that we can subsequently use them without adding to the confusion.

First, it will be appropriate to discuss the computer itself. We can think of a computer as a very high speed mathematical technician who has been perfectly trained to solve some given type of problem using a certain procedure. This procedure has been so indelibly inscribed in the technician's memory that every time our technician is called upon to solve this problem using new data, he (or she, or it) goes about it in precisely the same manner, using exactly the same steps in the same order that was used the last time. To carry the analogy a step further, this technician's memory is of such a type that whenever the boss wants to, he can almost instantly erase all of the information (or any part of it, for that matter) in the technician's memory and quickly retrain the technician to solve another type of problem in a specific, predetermined and repeatable manner.

Internal Operation

The heart of the computing system is the processor whose memory consists of a large number of tiny magnetic elements called <u>bits</u> (the type and number are not the same for all computers) which can be magnetized in one direction or another. Such an element, able to operate in one of only two possible states, is said to be <u>bistable</u>. These two states are represented by "on" or "off," "yes" or "no," or most usually, 1 or 0. This allows a special code to be built into a computer's circuitry so that a piece of information (letter, number, or symbol) can be represented in the computer's memory as a unique combination of bits in the "on" status. This form of data representation is termed binary since strings of 1's and 0's represent quantities in a system in which the base is 2. More about this in Appendix A. Since we use a large number of different symbols for recording and communicating information, the unique representation of each type of character in a computer's memory requires several bistable bits. Consequently, computers must be designed to handle these bits in groups as well as singly. In fact, the instructions which enable a computer to operate with a single bit are used relatively infrequently compared with those referring to groups of bits. Standard conventions have been set up by designers for representing information in this manner. In such systems a group of bits treated as a unit which stores one character of information is called a byte. Although the number of bits per byte may vary with the type of computer, it is fixed by the circuit design for a given type. Two types of codes are used most widely, based on 6 and 8 bit bytes, respectively. These are shown in Tables A1 and A2 in Appendix A.

The memory elements in a computer may be interlinked further by additional circuitry which ties together a number of bytes. Such a combination, treatable as a unit, is called a word and computers are typed as being fixed word length or variable word length, depending on whether the number of bytes which can be logically linked in this fashion can or cannot be varied. The word, rather than the byte or bit, is considered to be the basic unit of memory. This may refer to a single byte, which is the smallest possible word in a variable word length computer, or a group of two, six, eight, or more bytes depending on the model of the fixed word length computer. Each word has a permanent location number or address assigned to it as part of the basic machine design. Whenever a computer is instructed to refer to the 1274th word in memory, for example, it will always examine the same word. Thus the computer is capable of storing, locating, and accessing coded information which may represent data or instructions. The amount of information which can be stored in memory at any one time gives us a criterion for assessing a computer's size. Computers capable of storing the equivalent of up to 20,000 characters are usually considered "small;" 100,000 characters is the approximate limit for so-called "medium sized" computers, and large computers with 1,000,000-character memories already exist. The fact that a computer can refer to or access information, given its location, gives us a criterion for comparing computers' speeds. This is expressed in terms of the time it takes a computer to locate a word in memory and transmit its contents to some other part of memory (access time). In this regard we're talking about a times ranging from several hundred milliseconds (thousandths of a second) down to several hundred nanoseconds (billionths of a second).

Input - Output

Just as numbers, letters, and other characters are internally represented by uniquely coded symbols, they must also be coded onto some compatible medium before they can be transmitted to and stored in a computer's memory. Thus, raw data (handwritten numbers in notebooks, printed sheets from automatic recorders, completed questionnaires, etc.) are generally not suitable for direct entry to the computer. To effect such entry, the data are transferred to some compatible input medium from which the computer is designed to accept (read) information for interpretation and final conversion to coded magnetic impulses.

Input Media

The most widely used medium for this purpose is the familar punched card (Figure 1). Each card may be considered as a data sheet capable of accommodating up to 80 characters of information. Data are

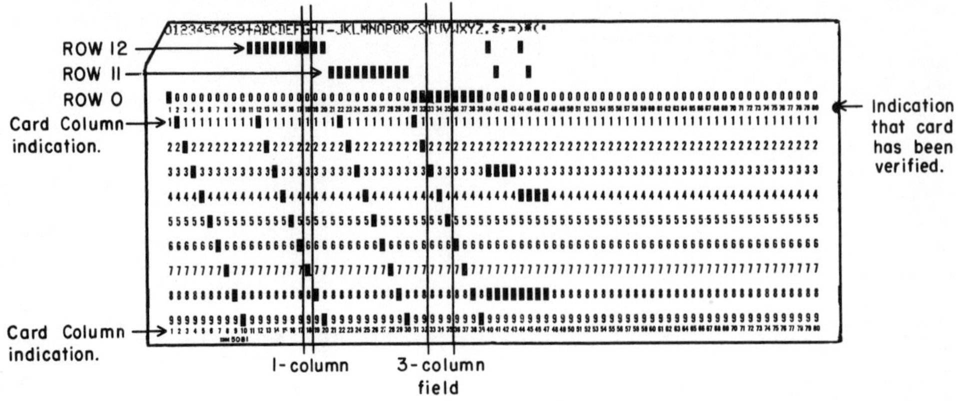

FIGURE 1
Standard Punched Card Showing Character Code

recorded on these cards by means of a keypunch (Figure 2) which is operated in much the same way as a typewriter and is designed to represent each standard character by a unique combination of punched holes. Once the cards are prepared, their contents are transmitted to the processor's memory via a card reader (Figure 3) which is electronically linked to it and operates in basically the same way as a player piano. A sensing mechanism causes certain circuits to be activated if certain combinations of holes exist and these circuits implant the proper information by setting the status of the appropriate bits in memory. The sensing mechanism may be electromechanical, taking the form of a set of metal brushes, or it may be photoelectric. Since the latter method involves fewer parts, it allows card reading to proceed faster than with brushes, and speeds as high as 2000 cards per minute have been reliably achieved.

FIGURE 2
Keypunch for Preparing Punched Cards

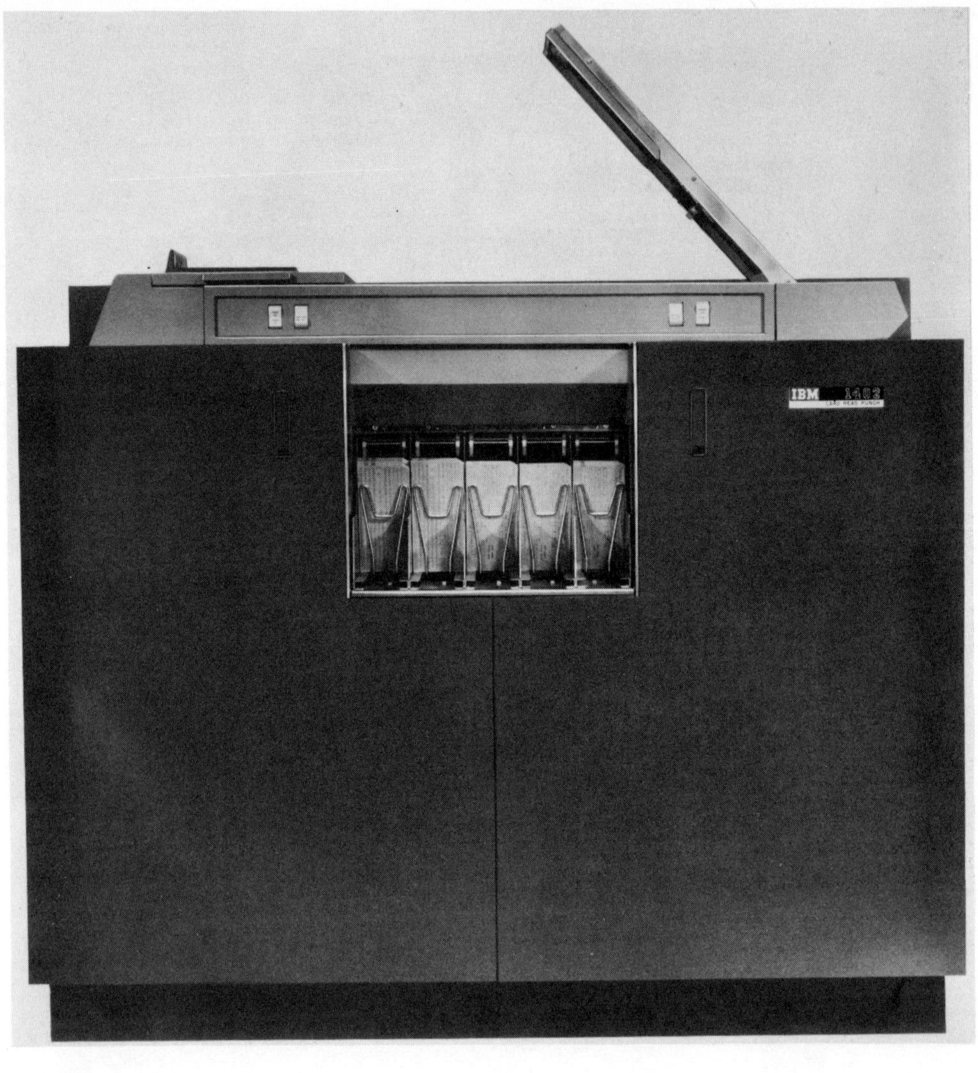

FIGURE 3
Card Reader

A similar medium is punched paper tape such as used with teletype equipment. Various codes are used to record information (two are shown in Figure 4), which is read by devices using electro-

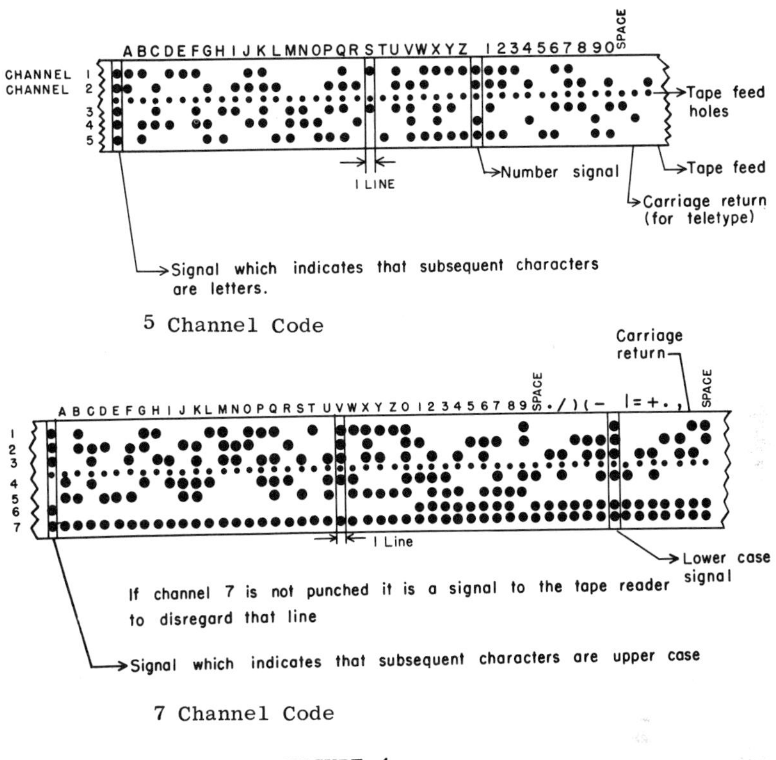

5 Channel Code

7 Channel Code

FIGURE 4
Punched Paper Tape Codes

mechanical or photoelectric sensors. This medium is not used frequently for manual recording of data. Instead it finds many applications as the recording end of a system in which data are being generated and collected automatically. When enough data are being produced to justify the cost involved in connecting a paper tape punch to a piece of data collection equipment, the slow and costly step of manually transcribing data onto a compatible input medium is eliminated. Other input media are available but less widely used.

Output Media

Once the computations and manipulation of data in the central processor are complete, the results must be reconverted to a form which is understandable to the user and must be presented on a medium which will supply him with a permanent copy, if he wishes one. The two most widely used devices for this purpose are the typewriter and high speed line printer (Figure 5). The former's use is usually limited to short messages because of its slow rate (maximum 15 characters per second). The latter, which produces an entire line of print at a time, is a highly versatile vehicle which, with proper persuasion, can be induced to print tables (Figure 6), graphs (Figure 7) or pictures (Figure 8). Present models can produce as many as 1500 lines of 132 characters each per minute. Other output devices are also available.

Magnetic Tape

Since the processor portion of a computing system is basically an electronic structure which operates with virtually no moving parts, the actual computations and manipulations can take place at a rate many times faster than that associated with the transmission of data to and from the processor. In fact the overall processing speed is often determined and limited by this transmission and the rate is said to be input-output bound.

Efforts to accelerate the input-output rate have resulted in the widespread acceptance of magnetic tape as the medium for direct use with computers. Its continuity and compactness in terms of data representation allow data transmission to and from tape at rates exceeding 50 times those obtained with card readers. As a result, many large computing systems are designed to be completely tape-oriented. Less expensive independent (off-line) equipment is used to prepare input tapes

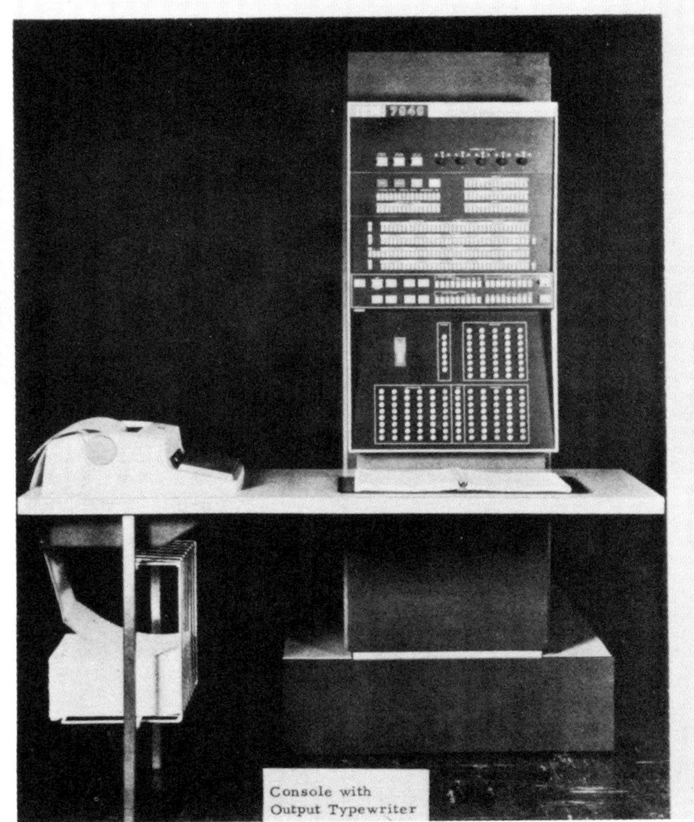

FIGURE 5
High Speed Line Printer and Console Typewriter

CINCINNATI NECPLASTIC DISEASE REGISTRY 1963

SITE	SLM	NO. DEAC	NO. MALE	NO. FEM.	W	C	UND. 2	2-15	16-30	31-40	41-50	51-60	61-70	OVER 70	DEF. SURG	RAD.	CHEM	STER	OTHER	NONE
PEN	3	0	3	0	2	1	0	0	0	0	1	0	1	1	3	0	0	0	0	0
KIC	39	15	25	14	32	7	1	2	0	1	7	11	13	4	29	6	3	0	0	8
URE	6	1	5	1	6	0	0	0	0	0	1	2	2	1	6	1	0	0	0	0
BLC	97	18	75	22	87	10	0	0	0	5	9	19	23	41	81	13	3	0	0	9
BLS	0	0	0	0	0	0	0	0	0	0	0	0	0	0	0	0	0	0	0	0
BLP	3	0	1	2	3	0	0	0	0	1	0	1	0	1	3	0	0	0	0	0
ETH	2	1	1	1	1	1	0	0	0	0	0	1	0	1	0	1	1	0	0	0
CST	11	1	5	6	9	2	0	2	1	3	2	0	1	2	10	3	2	0	0	0
RET	0	0	0	0	0	0	0	0	0	0	0	0	0	0	0	0	0	0	0	0
NML	19	3	12	7	19	0	0	0	1	2	4	6	3	3	14	3	3	0	0	3
BCN	5	0	3	2	5	0	0	1	0	0	2	0	1	1	3	1	0	0	0	1
BRN	54	27	36	18	50	4	5	4	3	6	11	12	8	5	39	25	2	1	1	7
MLY	50	17	34	16	47	3	0	4	4	10	5	6	10	11	2	24	18	5	4	16
LEU	54	24	37	17	49	5	2	8	5	1	6	8	16	8	0	6	33	23	22	12
MUL	12	4	5	7	7	5	0	0	0	0	1	1	5	5	0	4	7	2	0	2
EAR	0	0	0	0	0	0	0	0	0	0	0	0	0	0	0	0	0	0	0	0
EYM	0	0	0	0	0	0	0	0	0	0	0	0	0	0	0	0	0	0	0	0
EYR	2	0	2	0	2	0	1	1	0	0	0	0	0	0	2	0	0	0	0	0
EYS	0	0	0	0	0	0	0	0	0	0	0	0	0	0	0	0	0	0	0	0
THY	14	4	5	9	11	3	0	1	4	1	1	4	2	1	11	1	0	0	0	3
PTH	1	0	1	0	0	1	0	0	0	0	1	0	0	0	1	0	0	0	0	0
THM	1	0	1	0	1	0	0	0	1	0	0	0	0	0	0	1	0	0	0	0
ADR	2	2	2	0	2	0	0	0	0	1	1	0	0	0	1	2	0	0	0	0
PIT	7	3	5	2	6	1	1	0	2	1	1	0	1	1	3	2	0	0	0	3
PIN	1	0	1	0	1	0	0	1	0	0	0	0	0	0	1	1	0	0	0	0
MYF	0	0	0	0	0	0	0	0	0	0	0	0	0	0	0	0	0	0	0	0
SKI	127	4	70	57	123	4	0	1	2	7	23	25	32	37	114	10	0	0	1	4
LNC	115	61	63	52	97	18	0	0	2	3	14	33	39	24	1	30	19	2	0	71
MSG	11	0	3	8	9	2	0	0	2	4	1	3	1	0	11	0	0	0	0	0
GBT	0	0	0	0	0	0	0	0	0	0	0	0	0	0	0	0	0	0	0	0
HYC	2	0	0	2	1	1	0	1	1	0	0	0	0	0	1	0	0	0	0	1
MEN	12	4	4	8	8	4	0	0	1	1	1	4	4	1	8	0	0	0	0	4
PCL	2	0	1	1	1	1	0	0	0	0	0	2	0	0	0	0	1	0	1	0
PCM	22	0	0	22	12	10	0	0	6	11	3	2	0	0	15	0	0	0	0	7
TER	0	0	0	0	0	0	0	0	0	0	0	0	0	0	0	0	0	0	0	0
HIS	0	0	0	0	0	0	0	0	0	0	0	0	0	0	0	0	0	0	0	0
NFB	0	0	0	0	0	0	0	0	0	0	0	0	0	0	0	0	0	0	0	0

TOTAL NCN-MALIG. = 49
TOTAL MALIG. = 2152
2 PRI. SITES = 140
3 PRI. SITES = 10
3+ PRI. SITES = 2
GRAND TOTAL = 2201
REJECTED CARDS = 0

FIGURE 6

Tabular Output Produced on the Line Printer

```
PROJECT NO.        0000
INVESTIGATOR       DR. ANHEUSER BUSCH
AUGUST 30, 1962

                    SCATTERGRAM
        LIVER WEIGHTS VS. BODY WEIGHTS

                   CONTROL GROUP

          16.00 -
          14.00 -
          12.00 -
 LIVER
          10.00 -
 WEIGHT
           8.00 -
           6.00 -
           4.00 -
 SCALE
 0.40 PER LINE
       220.0  250.0  280.0  310.0  340.0  370.0  400.0  430.0  460.0  490.0

                    SCALE        3.0 PER SPACE
                       BODY WEIGHT

NUMBER OF PIECES OF DATA                                SYMBOL TABLE
  ENTERED          113      SYMBOL                .     •     X     /     O
  REJECTED                  NUMBERS INDICATED    1- 1  2- 2  3- 3  4- 4  5 OR MORE
  OUT OF ORDER
```

FIGURE 7

Graphical Output Produced on the Line Printer

FIGURE 8
Pictorial Output Produced on the Line Printer

(such as shown in Figure 9) or convert data on output tapes to readable form. This enables the large system to spend more of its available time doing actual computing. More information on magnetic tape is given in Appendix B.

Communication With Computers

Computers are designed to accept a certain number of very specific coded instructions. The code that a given type of computer accepts is called its machine language. A sequence of such instructions designed to do a given set of computations or perform some other problem-solving function is called a program. Since the computer cannot operate on a problem unless its memory contains the procedural instructions in proper sequence, we talk about stored programs and stored program computers. To shed further light on this, we can say that a desk calculator is a computer, but not of the stored program type. If we want to add two numbers together on a desk calculator, we enter the first number, add it in, enter the second number, then add it to the first. By operating this way, we do the actual remembering. In contrast to this, the stored program computer stores the two numbers in its memory. It also stores the instruction to add them together. Thus we do not enter a piece of data and press the ADD button. Instead we activate the computer, enabling it to carry out the instructions stored in its memory, operating on the specified data also stored in its memory. The result of the addition will be stored in the computer's memory as well. This brings us to the task of providing a set of properly defined, correctly sequenced instructions for getting data into the computer's memory where it can be processed to produce the required results (output), and getting these results out of the computer's memory and into a form such that people can look at, understand and use them. This lofty pursuit is called

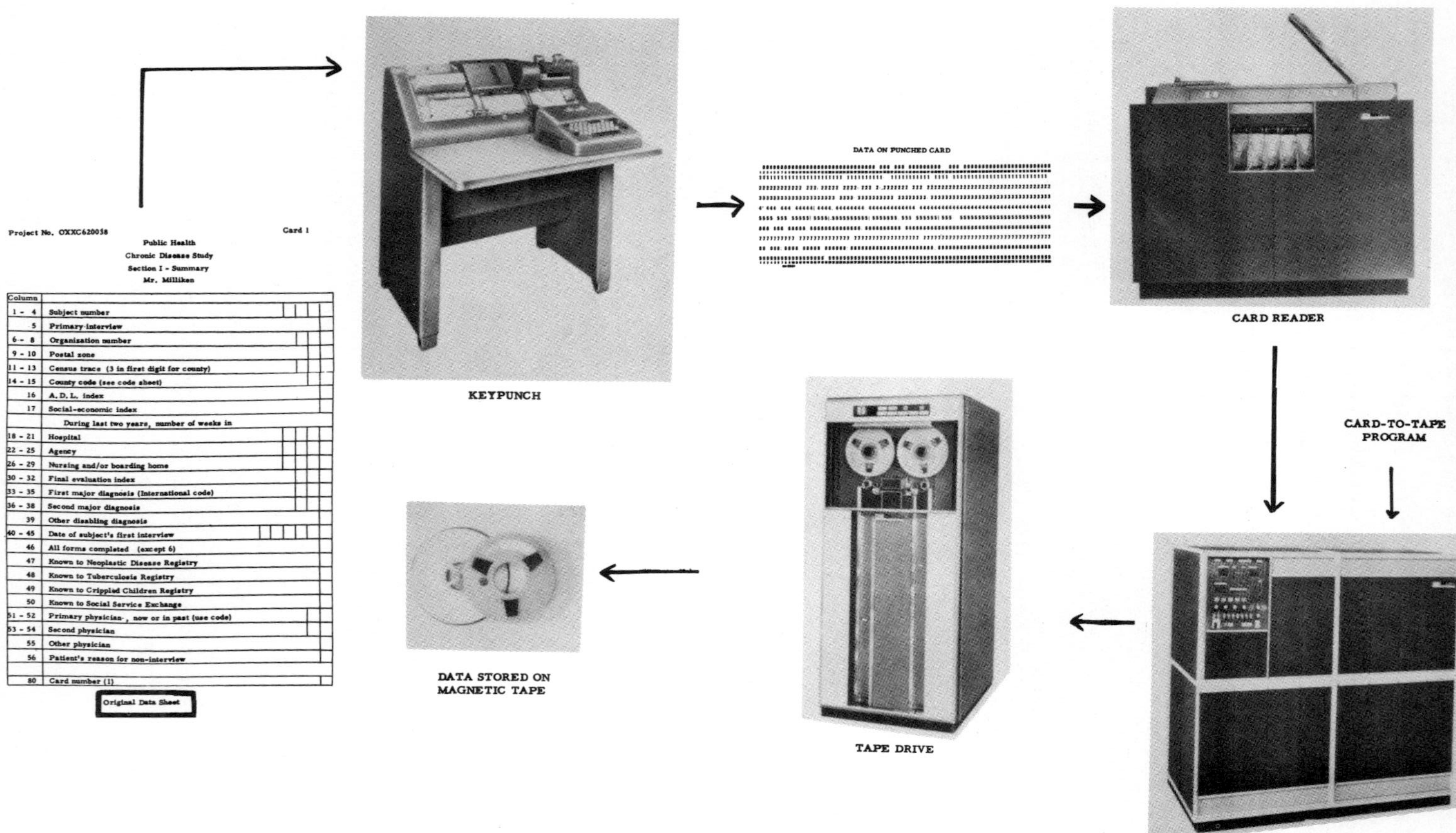

FIGURE 9
Flow of Information in a Card-to-tape Data System

programming and the pursuant (or pursued?) is a programmer or computernik.

Let us now examine the sequence of events that must take place if we are to take advantage of our ferromagnetic technician's high speed, perfect memory and totally predictable habits:

1. Raw data are transcribed onto some compatible input medium, as previously described.
2. The program is implanted in the computer's memory (loaded).
3. Once this is done, the computer begins to execute the instructions, one at a time. Data are called in (read) and used in various computational operations.
4. Once the program completes the production of results (output), it then provides for the output to be transferred to some suitable display medium.

Program Requirements

From this flow of events we can, by implication, develop a list or requirements a program must fulfill to allow successful processing:

1. It must, of course, have all of the proper steps, in correct sequence.
2. Provisions must be included for differentiating between instructions and data, since both types of information ultimately end up as combinations of magnetic impulses which could easily be taken for either type.
3. Orders of magnitude of the input must be recognized and accounted for, so that output magnitudes will be correct for the entire anticipated range of input values.

4. Provisions must be included for identifying runs (or jobs) where different sets of data (data files) are being processed using the same program.
5. Output must be properly arranged and labeled so that the observer, looking at the printed copy, will encounter no ambiguity.

Thus we can see that in addition to the actual mathematical steps involved in performing calculations, the program includes a number of logical steps, for manipulating data, whether they be input, output or intermediate results. It will behoove us to keep this in mind as we go on, since manipulative operations will invariably cause more trouble than computational ones. This is true because a program for solving a given type of problem cannot be developed (written) until the exact method of solution is known precisely and in great detail. Hence the computational part of the program is already, for all practical purposes, worked out.

Preparation of Programs

In almost any field of endeavor it is often necessary to depict the flow of events in a concise form which clearly and quickly conveys to the reader a summary of what is taking place and in what order. In chemistry this might be a flowsheet indicating the steps in a chemical process; in medicine this could be a schematic diagram depicting the steps in a surgical procedure; in law such a summary could be used to trace the steps in the preparation of a case and its progress through the judicial system. In any event, such a graphical summary offers strong proof of the magnitude of the word-to-picture ratio discovered by the ancient Chinese.

This type of summary finds great use in data processing, where it is applied in two basic ways: One involves an overall schematic representation of the flow of information from the time it comes into a computing center as raw data to the time it leaves as finished output. As such, this type of schematic includes data preparation, keypunching, sorting, and all other steps peripheral to the actual computation. Processing by the computer is indicated as a single step in such a summary, which, incidentally, is called a flowchart. The type of schematic summary we're interested in at present is a more detailed look at the computer processing itself. Hence we're concerned with the flow of logic in a program and the order and type of computations performed. When such a summary (called a block diagram) is properly prepared it can be used in several ways:

1. When prepared by a researcher or programming supervisor it can effectively define the nature of a required program. The programmer who is actually going to work out the individual instructions can use this summary as a guide.
2. Once a program is coded (the individual instructions are written out) the programmer can use the summary as a check to make sure that nothing has been omitted. This can save a lot of time and trouble later on, when the program is being debugged.
3. The block diagram serves as a common medium for transposing programs from one machine to another. Suppose, for example, that an individual came upon a report about a program which had potential use for him or his computing center. Regardless of the language in which the actual program is written, its block diagram would allow the reconstruction of the program for his machine.

In setting down guidelines for the preparation of informative block diagrams, it will help to classify the types of operations performed by computers. In addition to clarifying the connection between the block diagram and the program it represents, such a summary will reemphasiz the basic functional capabilities of computers.

1. The first general category includes all the basic internal operations performed on data. That is, all the mathematical computations, counting, and moving information from one part of memory to another.

2. All the operations which involve the transmission of informatio to and from the central processor (input-output instructions) from another general category. These instruct the computer as to what type of data are being transmitted, where they come from, and where they are going.

3. The third basic type of computer operation, and, incidentally, the most intriguing by far, is the decision function. Here the computer compares pieces of data and chooses one of a number of alternate activities based on the outcome of this comparison. With these basic functions in mind, we can turn to the actual architecture of block diagram

Symbols used in block diagrams vary in number and type. We'll use a fairly standard set consistent with the amount of detail we're going to express. It must be realized of course, that some happy medium must be found between a block diagram that lists each individual instruction and one which simply says

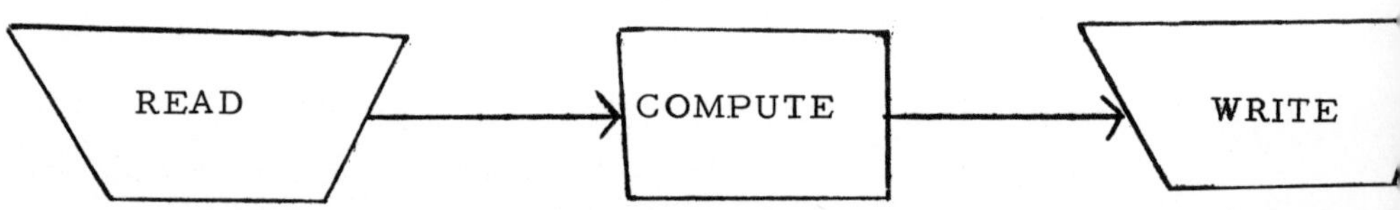

The first symbol is the connector which indicates the direction of the flow of logic. A straight line is used, with an arrow pointing to

the next step or group of steps:

Any processing which takes place in the computer is symbolized by a rectangle:

CALCULATE SQUARE
ROOT OF PRODUCT XY

A slot is used to symbolize any console operation. As such it is used mostly to indicate the beginning and end of a program, or intentional pauses in that program:

STOP

Input-output functions are symbolized by a trapezoid:

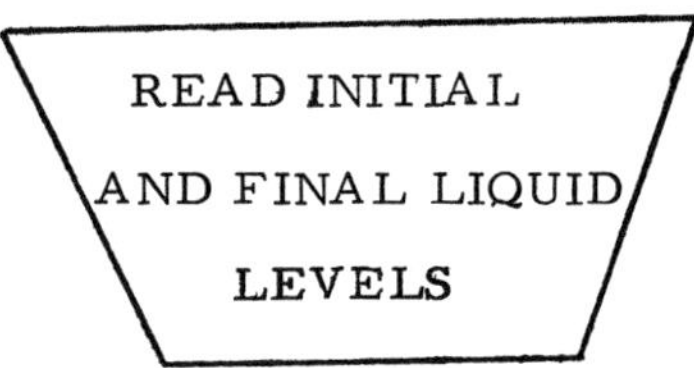

Decision functions in which the program can go in one of several directions are indicated by a rhombus:

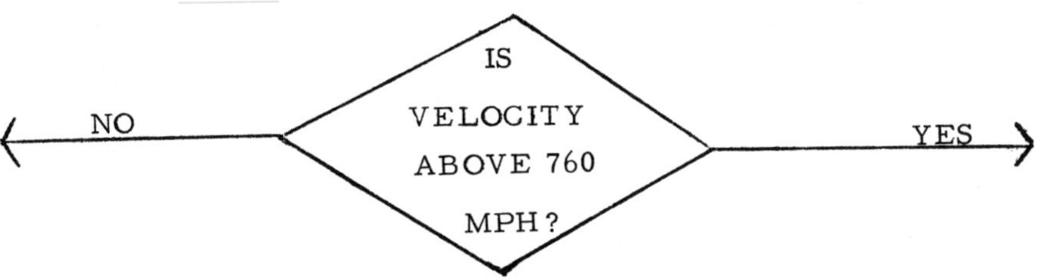

Circles are used in block diagrams to provide landmarks for connecting portions of the block diagram with corresponding steps in the program.

Thus the encircled 14 above indicates that the subsequent step in the block diagram corresponds to the section of the program beginning with statement number 14. Other more specific block diagram symbols are shown in Figure 10.

Languages for Programming

We mentioned coded instructions and machine language before. Each type of computer has built into its circuitry the ability to recognize certain combinations of magnetized bits in its memory. The action resulting from this recognition is, basically, a synthesis of a network of circuits whose end result corresponds to the execution of the instruction indicated by the bits.

Machine language instructions don't really tell the computer to do anything in the same direct sense as we usually think of it. For example an "ADD" instruction as machine language doesn't tell the computer to add anything to anything. Instead it instructs the computer to magnetize certain bits in a given word in memory. This combination will signal the logic circuitry to set up the appropriate network.

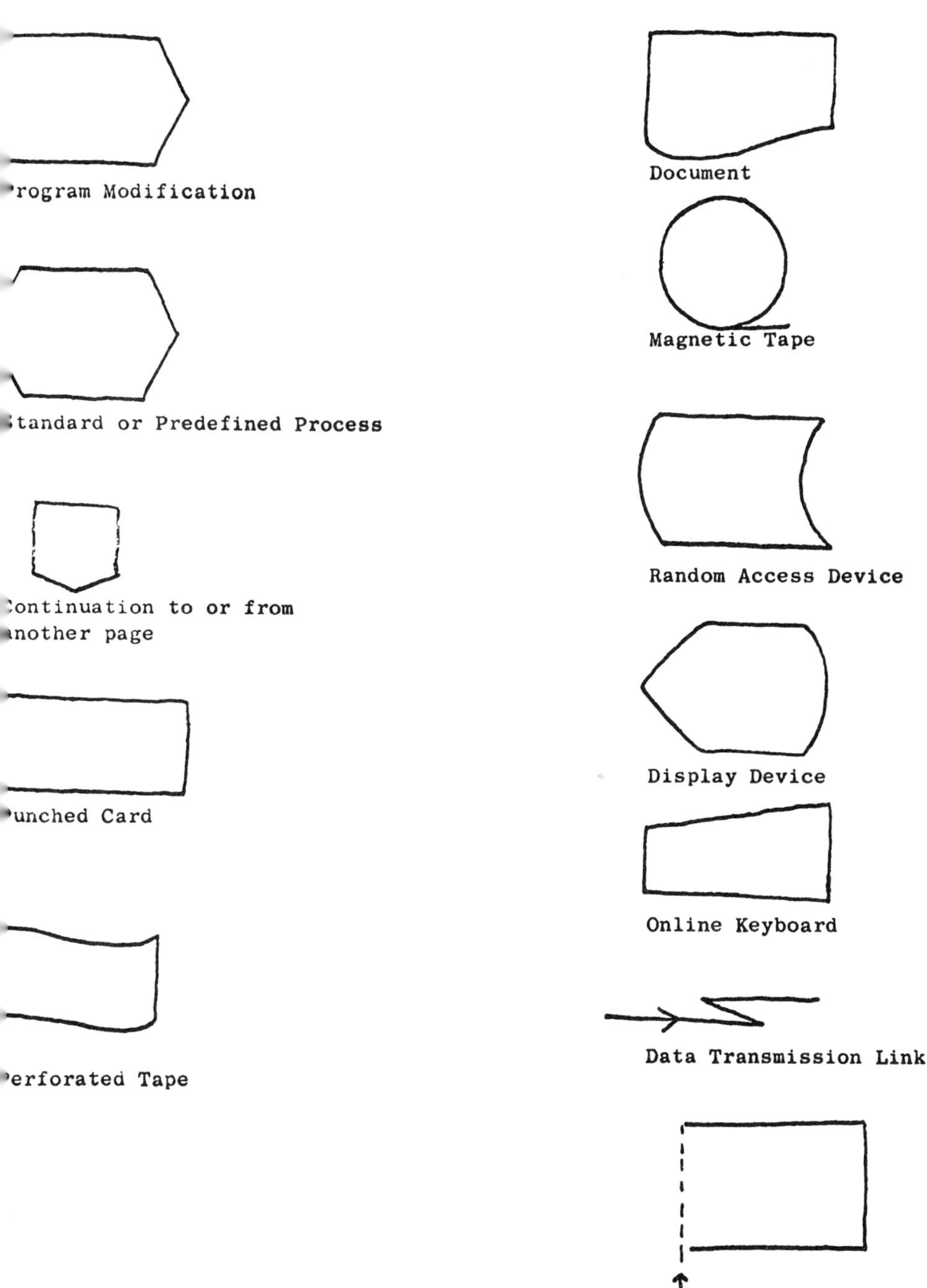

FIGURE 10

Additional Symbols Used in Flowcharting

Consequently, the code of a machine language instruction bears not even the slightest relation to the name of the intended instruction, thus making it very difficult to learn the code systematically. As an illustration, suppose we want to tell the machine the following:

"Add the number stored in address (or location) 12331 to the accumulator" (the accumulator is a special extra word in memory used in many machines as a standard place for carrying out certain operations). In machine language, the word in storage containing this instruction would look like this:

000100000000000000000011000000101011

where the 1's indicate those bits which have been magnetized in a certain direction and the zeros indicate those which have not.

If we were to write programs directly in machine language it would be necessary for us not only to be able to express each instruction in machine language but also to keep track of exactly where everything is stored, in terms of actual (<u>absolute</u>) storage locations. In the case of small programs this is merely a pain in the neck. With larger programs it becomes nearly impossible. Consequently, program languages have been devised to allow computerniks to write in a form more closely related to the spoken vernacular. Such languages may be divided roughly into two basic groups: Machine-oriented and problem-oriented types.

The first of these is written for a specific type of computer and as such supplies mnemonic counterparts for each machine language instruction. A special program, called an <u>assembler</u>, provides the go-between which produces machine language instructions from the mnemonic commands, assigns storage locations to instructions and data areas specified by the programmer and adds the required instructions for loading the program into the computer's memory. This sequence of events, together with appropriate terminology, is schematically depicted in Figure 11.

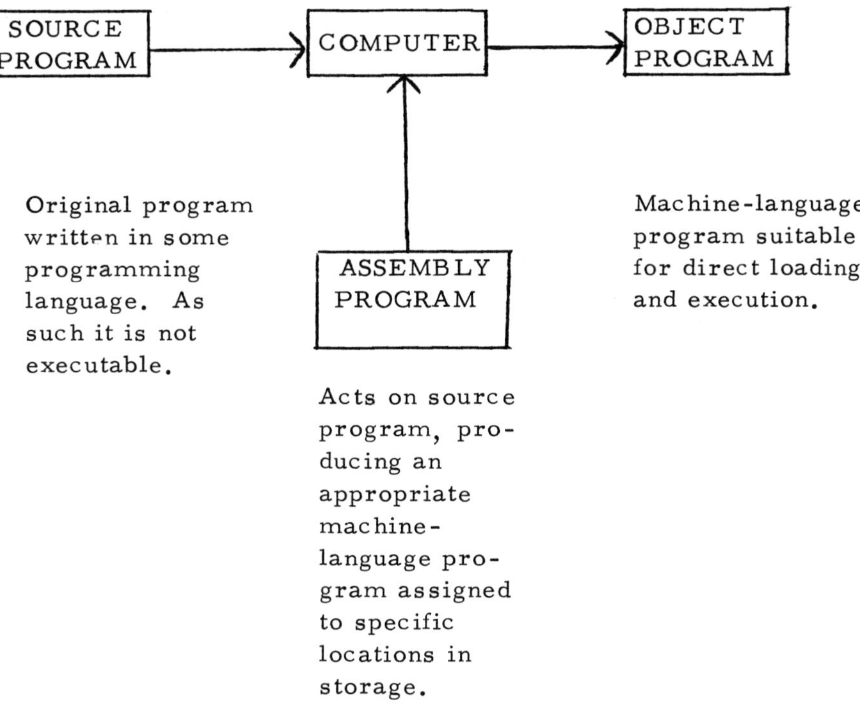

FIGURE 11

An assembly program performs another extremely valuable service. It eliminates the need for elaborate bookkeeping by allowing the programmer to assign names to areas in storage without having to know or care about the actual locations. Thus, in a previous example, we stated that the representation

000100000000000000000011000000101011

instigated the required electronic activity to allow the addition of the contents of location 12331 to the accumulator. To solidify our terminology we can now say that the instruction would appear in that form in an object program. The source program instruction that produced that mess of 1's and zeros might very well look like this:

ADD X

The programmer, let's say, is interested in adding X to something. He doesn't care where in memory X is. He wants to be able to call it X so that he can keep track of the logic more easily. The assembler lets the programmer do this by giving him the power to reserve areas in storage and assign names to these areas. Note the distinction here: When we usually talk about X we're referring to a variable which we've chosen to call X. When the computer "talks about X" it is referring to the address where the value of **X** is stored. So the source program instruction says: "Add the contents of the location designated 'X' to someplace." Since computers with accumulators usually have only one "someplace" where addition may take place, this need not be specified. When the assembler encounters this instruction it will generate the machine-language equivalent of ADD, determine which location it had assigned to X and substitute that location number for X. Thus the object deck will contain only actual addresses. Special programs are always available which produce side-by-side listings of source and object programs for cross-referencing when this is required.

The second type of programming language goes several steps beyond the type just described. In general the basic language is not written for exclusive use with any one machine. Instead, general rules and concepts are formulated which define the orientation of the language and how it is to be used. Here we're talking about problem orientation. The purpose of this type of language is to provide powerful instructions which will simplify the programming of some given broad category of problem solutions. For example, one such language might be designed for insurance use, another for banking applications, a third for automatic language translators, etc. Once the basic rules are defined, appropriate programs can be written to allow the programmer to use this language on his type of computer. Such programs are called compilers and differ from assemblers in that in almost all cases an instruction from the source program to the compiler necessitates the generation of several machine language instructions to carry out the intended operation. Thus, these languages take the programmer further away from the machine and move him closer to the problem he is working on. The action of the compiler is shown in Figure 12.

Rules for FORTRAN

Of the many problem-oriented languages presently in existence, FORTRAN (short for FORmula TRANslation) is probably the most well known. It was developed by a group of people from various industries for use with scientific and engineering problems. FORTRAN compilers are available for many different types of computers. The version with which we shall be working is the most recent and is called FORTRAN IV. As we go through its characteristics and rules it will be seen that the language allows the programmer to write equations and expressions in very much the same way he would when doing calculations manually.

The basic instruction in FORTRAN is called the statement. Each statement deals with some aspect of the problem being solved and

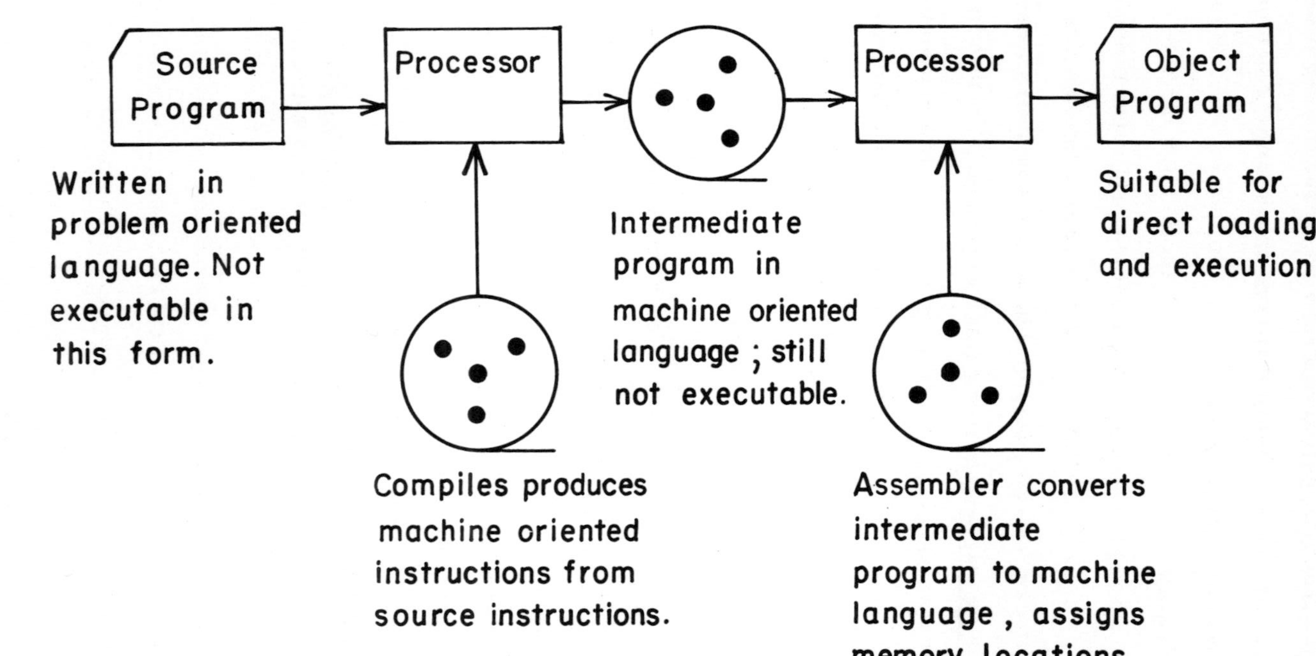

FIGURE 12

Schematic Diagram Showing Action of a Compiler

may call for computation, logical decisions, data manipulation or other operations. FORTRAN source programs are usually written on and keypunched from specially prepared coding sheets, such as shown in Figure 13. Information from these forms is transcribed onto punched cards of the type shown in Figure 14. Rules for using the sheets are described below:

1. It is good practice to sprinkle programs liberally with comments. These are remarks which are ignored by FORTRAN (just reproduced as they are) and serve as guideposts in the logical sequence. This not only keeps the programmer from getting lost but helps others to understand and therefore use his program effectively. Let's illustrate the use of comments in a schematic example:

Statements	A group of statements handling some section of a procedure
Comment	AT THIS POINT X AVERAGE HAS BEEN CALCULATED
Statements	Another group of statements representing some further processing
Comment	X AVERAGE HAS BEEN COMPARED TO Y AND THE HIGHER VALUE WILL BE USED TO FIND Z
	Etc.

Comments may go anywhere in a program, since they are not processed. FORTRAN recognizes comments cards by

FORTRAN CODING FORM

		Punching Instructions		Page of
Program		Graphic	Card Form # *	Identification 73 80
Programmer	Date	Punch		

C FOR COMMENT

STATEMENT NUMBER | Cont. | FORTRAN STATEMENT

1 5 6 7 10 15 20 25 30 35 40 45 50 55 60 65 70 72

COMMENTS MAY START HERE AND MUST HAVE "C" IN COLUMN 1

ALL SOURCE STATEMENTS MUST START HERE

DO NOT KEYPUNCH PAST COLUMN 72

THIS COLUMN USED ONLY FOR CONTINUED SOURCE STATEMENTS

CCOMMENTS MAY BE STARTED IN COLUMN 2 AND CAN EXTEND UP TO COLUMN 72----.

C FOR COMMENT | STATEMENT NUMBER | CONTINUATION | FORTRAN STATEMENT | IDENTIFICATION

ALL SOURCE STATEMENTS BEGIN IN COLUMN 7.

C FOR COMMENT | STATEMENT NUMBER | CONTINUATION | FORTRAN STATEMENT | IDENTIFICATION

IBM 888157

FIGURES 13 and 14

Representation of FORTRAN Source Program on Coding Sheet and Punched Card the "C" in the first column, which they alone contain. If a card is not a comment card, column 1 may not contain a C. The comment itself is given in column 2 - 72. For long-winded comments additional comment cards are used.

2. Each line represents one punched card. Columns 1 - 5 are available for numbering statements. This turns out to be extremely useful since it provides the programmer with a means of referencing statements without knowing any actual locations. Statement numbers must be numeric (no letters or symbols allowed). No decimals are used and statements need not be numbered in any order or sequence. Effort should be made to restrict the numbered statements to those referred to by other statements in the program. Since the compiler accumulates a complete list of statement numbers as part of its analysis of the source program, the speed and efficiency of compilation are both adversely affected by excessive use of statement numbers. Computing time is a parameter much worried about by administrators, who are fond of expressing the monthly rental cost as dollars per minute or even per second.

3. The actual statement begins in column 7 and may go as far as 72. If additional length is required, the statement may be continued on a number of additional line depending on the particular type of computer. Table I shows the limits on continued for various computers. Although continuation numbers need not be consecutive,it is a good practice to use consecutive numbering (such as 0 - 9,

then A, B, C, etc.). FORTRAN looks for a number other than zero in column 6 to see whether a particular line is a continuation of the statement on the previous line. Thus, column 6 is used only for denoting continuation of a statement. Otherwise it is left blank. Only one statement goes on a line.

TABLE I

Limitations on Continuation Cards for FORTRAN Statements

Type of Computer	Maximum Number of Continuation Cards
IBM 360, 7090, 7094, RCA Spectra 70	19
IBM 1401, 1410, 1440, 1460	9
UNIVAC III, RCA 3301	9
CDC 3200	4
CDC 3400, 3600	No limit *
PHILCO 2000	20

*The FORTRAN compilers impose a limit on the number of operations in a given statement (598).

4. Columns 73 - 80 are available for any identifying information (such as the program name or number).
5. FORTRAN ignores blanks except in column 6 or in FORMAT statements (discussed later). Thus, blanks may be used to increase clarity and legibility. For example, the statement

```
X = SQRT(A**2+B**2+4.7*C)
```

can be legitimately replaced by

```
X = SQRT (A**2 + B**2 + 4.7*C)
```

6. All alphabetic information is printed as capital letters. For purposes of standardization, the following conventions have been set up:

   The letter between H and J is written I, to distinguish it from the number 1.

   The last letter of the alphabet is written Ƶ, to distinguish it from the number 2.

   The letter between N and P is written Ø, to distinguish it from zero.

   Between P and R comes Q

   A lower case b indicates one blank space.

Figure 15 shows a program segment written on the standard coding sheet.

FORTRAN CODING FORM

Program: DØSE INTENSITY
Programmer: YØINEH SCHIMMEL
Date: 9/15/64
Punching Instructions — Graphic / Punch — Card Form #
Page 2 of 4
Identification: DØSE INT (columns 73–80)

C FOR COMMENT

STATEMENT NUMBER (1–5)	Cont. (6)	FORTRAN STATEMENT (7–72)
		IF(AP(I).GT.0.)GØ TØ 120
		RAP=0.
		GØ TØ 125
120		RAP=ALØG10(AP(I))
125		X=(0.0056-0.013*D(J))/(1.-0.0056+0.013*D(J))
		Y=(0.036*D(J)-2.044)/(1.-0.0056+0.013*D(J))
		TC=(2.044-0.036*D(J)+(0.013*D(J)-0.0056)*RAP)
		CI=10.0*TC
		IF(CI.GT.0.)GØ TØ 140
		RCI=0.
		GØ TØ 145
140		RCI=ALØG10(CI)
145		T=(ELL(K)-1.)/(0.17*SQRT(2.))
		R=(1.+0.278393*ABS(T)+0.230389*(T**2)+0.000972*ABS(T**3)+0.078108)
	1	*T**4))**4

FIGURE 15

A Portion of a FORTRAN Source Program Written on a Standard Coding Sheet

Chapter II

Constants, Variables, and Expressions

FORTRAN allows the programmer to define and use constants and variables in pretty much the same way as that used in ordinary mathematical notation.

Constants

Just as in mathematical context, a constant is some number whose value does not change from one run of the program to the next. For example, in the equation

NFEET = 5280 x MILES

5280 is a constant. There are five types of constants in FORTRAN IV.

1. Integer (Fixed Point) Constants

An integer constant is written without a decimal point and with or without a sign in front of it. (An unsigned number will be taken as positive.) The magnitude which such a constant may reach is different for various computers, as summarized in Table II. This type of number is called "fixed point because the decimal point, though not written, is always to the right of the rightmost digit.

Examples of valid integer constants are:

-3
0
17
+29
1194
-20015

Table II

Allowable Ranges for Integer Constants

Computer Type	Maximum Allowable Value	Number of Digits
IBM 360, RCA SPECTRA 70	$2^{15} - 1$	1 - 5
IBM 7040, 7044, 7090, 7094	$2^{35} - 1$	1 - 11
IBM 1401, 1410, 1440, 1460	$10^{20} - 1$	1 - 20 *
UNIVAC III	$10^{6} - 1$	1 - 6
SDS 9300	$10^{7} - 1$	1 - 7
RCA 3301	$10^{7} - 1$	1 - 7
CDC 3400, 3600	$2^{47} - 1$	1 - 15
CDC 3200	8388608	1 - 7
PHILCO 2000	2^{39}	1 - 12

*May be specified by the user for each program. If not specified a limit of 5 digits (maximum value of 99999) is automatically imposed.

2. Real (Floating Point) Constants

This is a number written with a decimal point (THIS IS A MUST). As in the case of integer constants, real numbers must be signed if negative and need not have a + sign in front of them if positive. Even if a number is an integer (like the number 4, for example) it makes a difference as to whether that number is written as 4 or 4.0. Although these have the same magnitude, their coded representation in the computer's memory is quite different. We shall see how this difference is utilized in subsequent sections.

Non-Exponential Forms

There are several valid forms for expressing real constants. These are best described by illustration, as shown below:

```
 18.74
-18.
+26.0
   .61
  0.077
```

"Floating point " indicates that there is no preset location for the decimal point.

Exponential Forms

This method of recording real constants is very close to scientific notation and at the same time approximates the form in which the constant is represented in memory. When the FORTRAN compiler comes across a real constant in a program, it breaks up that constant into two portions: A fractional portion and an exponent. The word of memory to which this value is transmitted is also treated in this manner. A certain number of bits standardly contain the fractional value and others contain a value representing the power of

10 by which that fraction must be multiplied to obtain the proper magnitude. Thus, for example, the storage of 47.2 could be represented schematically as

Fractional portion	Exponent portion
.472	+ 2

which says, in effect, "Multiply .472 by 10 to the + 2 power (or 100) to obtain the proper value." (In some computers the exponent portion precedes the fractional portion but the end result is the same.)

The following exponential forms are acceptable:

6.7E2	(interpreted as 6.7×10^{2})
6.0E+4	(interpreted as 6.0×10^{4})
+4.E03	(interpreted as 4.0×10^{3})
7.E-2	(interpreted as 7.0×10^{-2})
3.0E-03	(interpreted as 3.0×10^{-3})
4.E003	would not be valid because of the excess digit in in the exponent

Thus, for example, 6.7E2 could have been written as

```
+6.7E+02
 6.7E02
 6.70E02
67.E+1
 0.067E4
6700.E-1
670.
```

All of these would be represented exactly the same way in memory. As is the case with integer constants, there are limits to the number of digits and magnitudes of real constants. These depend on a given computer's internal characteristics and the design of the FORTRAN compiler for that particular machine (see Table III).

Table III

Allowable Ranges for Real Constants

Computer Type	Allowable Range	Number of digits
IBM 360, RCA SPECTRA 70	10^{-75} to 10^{75} -10^{-75} to -10^{75} and 0.	1 - 7
IBM 7040, 7044, 7090, 7094	10^{-38} to 10^{38} -10^{-38} to -10^{38} and 0.	1 - 9
IBM 1401, 1410, 1440, 1460*	10^{-100} to $(1-10^{18}) \times 10^{99}$ -10^{-100} to $-(1-10^{18}) \times 10^{99}$ and 0.	1 - 18
UNIVAC III	10^{-51} to 10^{49} -10^{-51} to -10^{49} and 0.	1 - 10
SDS 9000	10^{-77} to 10^{77} -10^{-77} to -10^{77} and 0.	1 - 12
RCA 3301	10^{-100} to $(1-10^{-8}) \times 10^{99}$ -10^{-100} to $-(1-10^{-8}) \times 10^{99}$ and 0.	1 - 8
CDC 3200	10^{-308} to 10^{308} -10^{-308} to -10^{308} and 0.	1 -10
CDC 3400, 3600	10^{-308} to 10^{308} -10^{-308} to -10^{308} and 0.	1 -11
PHILCO 2000	10^{-616} to 10^{616} -10^{-616} to -10^{616} and 0.	1 - 11

* As specified by the user for each program. A limit of 8 digits is automatically set if no specification is given.

If the allowable number of digits is exceeded, FORTRAN will disregard the rightmost excess digits. Thus, in a machine with an eight digit limit, for example, the value

41.27689076

will be stored as

+.	4	1	2	7	6	8	9	0	+02

Note that the two least significant digits (the 76) are just ignored, without rounding. If, through some calculation or by some error, a floating point number should turn up which lies outside of the range of values allowed by the FORTRAN compiler for a given machine, a condition exists known as overflow or underflow, depending on which end of the range is exceeded. The result of this condition depends on the particular machine being used. Some will cause a special message to be printed while others will terminate processing altogether.

3. Double-Precision Constants

The limitations on the number of significant digits allowed for constants in a given machine are determined in great part by the internal memory structure of each type of computer. Thus, if a degree of precision is required beyond that inherent in the machine's basic design, special instructions must be built into the compiler for providing this precision. The term "double precision" is used to indicate that two words are treated as a single logical entity. The allowable range of magnitude is usually not changed.

In the non-exponential form, a double precision constant is written in a form no different from that used by single precision values, except that there are more digits. Hence, for example, a FORTRAN compiler for a given machine accepting 14 digits will allow a constant such as

316.17492668165

to be transmitted into memory. When a FORTRAN compiler is provided with this capability it will, of course, not truncate a value whose precision (number of significant digits) exceeds the single-precision limit. Instead, it will automatically assume it is a double precision number and store it appropriately.

In the exponential form, replacement of the E with a D lets FORTRAN know that the number is to be stored as a double precision value, occupying two words of memory. The following are valid double precision constants in exponential form:

```
 6.7D2
-6.0D+4
+4.D03
 7.D-2
 3.0D-03
```

Table IV shows the double precision limits for computers whose FORTRAN compilers contain this capability.

Table IV

Allowable Ranges for Double Precision Constants

Computer Type	Number of Digits
IBM 360, RCA SPECTRA 70	1 - 16
IBM 7040, 7044, 7090, 7094	1 - 17
CDC 3400, 3600	1 - 25
PHILCO 2000	1 - 21

Machines not listed above do not have this feature.

4. Complex Constants

In many scientific areas, there are occasions when certain computations yield results which appear to violate some basic rules in mathematics. As an example let us consider the quadratic equation

$$X^2 + 8X + 25 = 0$$

When we substitute in the quadratic formula we obtain the two roots of this equation as follows:

$$X_1 = \frac{-B + \sqrt{B^2 - 4AC}}{2A} = \frac{-8 + \sqrt{64 - 4(1)(25)}}{2(1)}$$

$$X_2 = \frac{-B - \sqrt{B^2 - 4AC}}{2A} = \frac{-8 - \sqrt{64 - 4(1)(25)}}{2(1)}$$

or $\quad X_1 = \dfrac{-8 + \sqrt{-36}}{2}$ and $X_2 = \dfrac{-8 - \sqrt{-36}}{2}$

The rules governing algebraic multiplication stipulate that a product of two numbers having like signs must be positive, thus precluding such a thing as the square root of a negative number. Since such situations do come up and must be handled, the concept of imaginary numbers was introduced. A standard base value has been defined as $\sqrt{-1}$ and is called i. Thus $i^2 = -1$ and all imaginary numbers are referred to as multiples of i. Going back to the previous example, we can express the two imaginary roots as

$$X_1 = \frac{-8 + \sqrt{36}\sqrt{-1}}{2} = -4 + 3i$$

$$X_2 = \frac{-8 - \sqrt{36}\sqrt{-1}}{2} = -4 - 3i$$

It is seen that each root has a real part and an imaginary part. Numbers consisting of such combinations are called complex numbers and a whole set of rules regarding the mathematical manipulations of these quantities has been established, including conventions for graphical representation. (The reader is referred to any college algebra text for detailed discussion and derivations.)

In FORTRAN IV, complex constants are written inside parentheses with the real and imaginary portions expressed as legitimate floating point constants separated by a comma. Thus

- 4 + 3i is written (- 4., + 3.)
or (- 4.0, 3.0)

or any other acceptable form, exponential notation included. Some valid examples are given below:

Conventional Notation	FORTRAN
7.2 + 16.6i	(7.2, 16.6)
5280 - 247.4i	(.528E4 - 2474.E-1)
.0076 + .0002i	(7.6E - 03, 2.0E - 4)

(5280, 247.4) would not be valid, since the decimal point was not included in the real portion. Limitations on each of these constants are the same as those imposed on ordinary floating point values (as discussed in section 2 above).

Compilers for the following computers are not equipped with this capability: IBM 1401, 1410, 1440, and 1460; UNIVAC III.

5. Logical Constants

A rapidly increasing number of computer applications are developing in which the handling of non-numeric data (words, sentences, remarks, etc.) plays a crucial part. Consequently, FORTRAN IV has beeen given the capability of performing types of operations which are not computational in nature but, instead, deal with logical relations between pieces of information. Results of such operations are, therefore, not expressed as numbers. Rather, they reflect a condition of "truth" or "falsity" as defined by the particular problem. This will be treated in more detail when logical operations are discussed.

In general, a convention has been set up in FORTRAN IV wherein all logical quantities or operations are denoted by periods on either side of names or symbols. With regard to logical constants (there can be only two different values, i.e., "true" or "false") the forms are as follows:

```
.TRUE.
.FALSE.
```

6. Literal Constants

The FORTRAN IV compilers for some computing systems (such as the IBM 360, RCA Spectra 70 and CDC 3600) include capability for accepting combinations of letters, numbers and symbols (alphameric information) as constants.

For the IBM 360, these literal constants are specified by enclosing the information in apostrophes. Strings of characters so designated will be stored in memory as is and can be produced at some subsequent point in a program. The heading

'SUMMARY TABLE A3'

is an example of a literal constant. The maximum length of a literal constant allowed by the IBM 360 is 255 characters, including blanks. (NOTE: The apostrophe, produced as a 4-8 punch (see Figure 1) may be represented on some keypunch machines as a dash (-) or commercial AT sign (@).) Since FORTRAN IV looks for apostrophes to determine the beginning and end of a literal constant, the word ISN'T has to be written as 'ISN''T'.

The CDC 3600 FORTRAN IV compiler identifies literal constants by the prefix nH where n is the number of characters (including blanks) in the literal string and H stands for Hollerith, the name of the man who devised the punched card. Thus, the literal constant OPUS NUMBER 1 would be written

13HOPUS NUMBER 1

The value of n is limited to 120. Literal constants are stored in the CDC 3600 in groups of eight. Thus if n is not a multiple of eight, blanks are added to the right of the last specified character.

For literal constants having eight characters or less, CDC 3600 FORTRAN IV also allows the use of the form nR. If n is less than eight, zeroes are added to the left of the first character. If n exceeds eight, only the first eight characters are stored. The name AURORA 7, for example, would be specified as 8RAURORA 7.

Variables

As is the case in mathematical notation, a variable is a quantity whose value is subject to change depending upon some specified conditions. The type of variables acceptable to FORTRAN IV are described below:

1. Integer (Fixed Point) Variables

These are variables whose values will always be integers (such as counters, patient numbers, subscripts). FORTRAN has certain rules governing the naming of these variables:

A. Names are limited to 6 digits or less, the first of which must be a letter. Numbers may appear in the middle of a name but there is to be no special character anywhere. (That includes embedded blanks.)

B. The first letter of an integer variable must be I, J, K, L, M, or N. (Ways of breaking this rule will be shown later.)

The following are valid names for integer variables:

JOB4
KOOK2
N
M2
KOUNT
LOOKNC

The following are unacceptable names for integer variables:

SMIN (begins with wrong type letter)
8JNL (begins with number)

KASH $	(contains special character)
MAX/MN	(contains special character)
I MN	(contains special character)
KLASSC1	(too long)

If the programmer wants some integer variable to have a meaningful name which begins with the wrong kind of letter or vice versa he usually adds a proper one. Thus

SPEED becomes NSPEED.

The numerical limits on integer variables are the same as those for integer constants.

2. Floating Point (Real) Variables

The naming of these is governed by the same rules as fixed point variables with the exception that their names must begin with a letter of the alphabet other than I, J, K, L, M, or N. Limits on magnitude are the same as those set for real constants.

3. Double Precision Variables

These are named the same way as single precision real variables and are differentiated from them only by their values. That is, if some double-precision value is initially assigned to a variable, FORTRAN will reserve two words of memory for that variable and all subsequent values which the variable may take on will be treated in this way. Identification is also effected by a TYPE statement, discussed later.

4. Complex Variables

The rules set down for the naming of real variables also apply here. Recognition of a variable as being complex occurs by examination of the form (described under "complex constants") or by declaring that a certain name refers to a complex variable in a TYPE statement.

5. Logical Variables

As in the case of logical constants, there are only two possible values which logical variables may assume (. TRUE. or FALSE.). Their naming follows no set of rules as such. It is, instead, the TYPE statement which distinguishes logical variables from the other types. More about this later.

Problems

1. Select the incorrect integer constants:

   a) -186

   b) 18, 407

   c) 19. 2

   d) 24

   e) 0

   f) -41.

   g) +9

   h) 17.0

2. Select the incorrect single precision floating point constants:

   a) -4. 2

   b) 7E2

   c) +3. 7E+5

   d) . 7

   e) 4

   f) -18. 0E41

   g) 376. 59720407

   h) -7. E-13

3. Express the following numbers as integer constants:

a) 7.E2

b) -16.0E-1

c) 29.4

d) 11.

e) .714

4. Express the following numbers as floating point constants:

a) 16

b) -243561

c) 612040

d) 186000000000

e) 10^{24}

5. Express the following numbers as double precision constants:

a) -0.06

b) 12

c) 4,624,967.22

d) 2.763009

e) 10^{41}

f) -3

6. Express the following quantities in FORTRAN:

a) $6 - 4i$

b) $\sqrt{-256}$

c) $12i$

d) $3.6 + \sqrt{-121}$

e) $-\sqrt{64}$

7. Select the illegal integer variables:

   a) NUMBERS
   b) MAXF
   c) COUNTN
   d) IMAX
   e) 123S
   f) J $ 44
   g) N55
   h) IMAX. 4

8. Select the illegal real variables:

   a) SOCK4
   b) SNMAX
   c) KLASSB
   d) 23CD
   e) COM*ST
   f) NUMBER
   g) S4420
   h) JS45

Expressions

Expressions are sequences of constants and/or variables linked by symbols which indicate a series of mathematical or logical operations. As in the case of constants and variables these expressions must follow a set of fairly strict rules. The two basic types of expressions handled in FORTRAN are arithmetic and logical. Rules for each type are discussed below.

Arithmetic Expressions

The following symbols are used for arithmetic operations:

Symbol	Function
+	Addition
-	Subtraction
*	Multiplication
/	Division
**	Exponentiation

These symbols must always be included. They cannot be implied as in conventional mathematical notation. The expressions XY or X (Y) in conventional notation might imply the product of X times Y. In FORTRAN IV, however, XY would merely be treated as a single variable named XY and X (Y) would be used as the function X of Y. The product X times Y must always be written X * Y. Other rules for constructing arithmetic expressions are given below:

a) All elements in an expression involving +, -, *, or / must be of the same mode (either real or integer). Thus, for example, if one wishes to add 3 to a real variable called B, the expression B + 3. or 3. + B must be used. B + 3 is illegal. This means that single precision, double precision, and complex constants and variables can be used in a single expression in any combination. Fixed point quantities (integers) are used only with other integers. There are some compilers which allow mixed mode expressions. These will be discussed later.

b) Modes may be mixed when using the exponentiating operation in the following manner:

1. Real numbers (single or double precision) may be raised to real or integer powers. Thus

B** 2. and B **2 are both legitimate FORTRAN representations of B^2

3.7D4 ** 3.1 is a valid expression for $37000^{3.1}$

3.7E4 ** 3 is a valid expression for 37000^3

2. Complex and fixed point numbers may be raised only to integer powers. Only real and double precision quantities may be raised to double precision exponents.

(3., 4.) ** 2 is all right,
(3., 4.) ** 2.5 is not.
I**3 is all right,
I**3.2 is not.

c) Logical constants or variables may not be used in an arithmetic expression.

d) When FORTRAN encounters an arithmetic expression, it uses a standardized hierarchy in performing the various calculations:

1. Exponentiation (**).

2. After exponentiation, if present, multiplications and divisions (* and /) are performed, left to right.

3. Following multiplication and division, additions and subtractions (+ and -) are performed, also from left to right.

Thus the expression

A * X ** 2 + B * X - C/D

would cause FORTRAN to set up the following sequences of operations:

<u>Step 1:</u> Calculate X^2

<u>Step 2:</u> Multiply X^2 by A

<u>Step 3:</u> Multiply X by B

<u>Step 4:</u> Divide C by D

<u>Step 5:</u> Add the product BX to AX^2

<u>Step 6:</u> Subtract C/D from the sum of AX^2 and BX

e) The hierarchy may be altered in a given expression by the use of parentheses. For example, the expression X + Y/Z + W is <u>not</u> equivalent to $\frac{X + Y}{Z + W}$ but rather to $X + \frac{Y}{Z} + W$. In keeping with the established hierarchy, Y/Z would first be computed, the result added to X and that sum added to W. If we rewrote the expression adding parentheses, viz. (X + Y)/(Z + W), the hierarchy would be reversed such that the operation within each set of parentheses was carried out first. Similarly, A + B * C - D is not equivalent to (A + B) (C - D) in algebraic notation. Instead, it would give the result obtained from A + (B C) - D. With parentheses, however, (A + B) * (C-D) is equivalent to (A + B) (C - D). Note that the FORTRAN multiplication symbol (*) cannot be omitted. (Some compilers accept expressions like (X + Y) (A + B) in place of (X + Y) * (A + B). However, since this is exceptional, it is best to always include the symbols.)

Most FORTRAN IV compilers process arithmetic expressions from left to right, thus assuming the implied presence of parentheses. There are exceptions, however, thus making it a good practice to eliminate ambiguity by using parentheses liberally. The IBM 360 FORTRAN, for example, which processes from left to right will treat the expression X ** Y** Z as if it were (X** Y) ** Z. The CDC 3600, on the other hand,processes from right to left and would treat this expression as if it were X** (Y ** Z). In all other compilers the expression X ** Y** Z will not be accepted without parentheses.

f) No two operation symbols may appear in succession. There must always be some constant or variable between these symbols. Thus for example, X * - Y is illegal.

Mixed Mode Arithmetic Expressions

More recent FORTRAN IV compilers, such as those designed for the IBM 360, CDC 3600/3400, and RCA Spectra 70 systems, allow the use of mixed modes in arithmetic expressions. This capability is provided by equipping the compiler with a set of routines which scan the expression and convert appropriate terms according to a pre-determined hierarchy so that the mode of the resulting value is defined. The hierarchy is as follows:

Complex
Double Precision
Real
Integer

Thus,the overall mode of an expression containing a complex constant or variable will be complex. Suppose C is a complex variable, X and Y are real variables, and J and K are integer variables. The expression

$$C * D ** 2/(X-Y) + J/K$$

would then be processed as follows:

1. The quantity (X - Y) is converted to complex form, and stored as (X - Y) + 0i (let's call it Z).

2. D^2 is evaluated and stored as the complex value $D^2 + 0i$ (call it W).

3. The value of C * W/Z is found (call it H).

4. J/K is evaluated, changed to a real value (say F) and converted to complex form F + 0i (call it G).

5. The final value, calculated of H + G, is stored as a complex quantity.

Similarly, the mode of an arithmetic expression containing no complex terms, but having one or more double precision terms, will be double precision.

Several other FORTRAN IV compilers, such as the Philco 2000, allow more limited mixed mode expressions in which real, double precision, and complex terms but not integers may appear together. In such cases, the hierarchy of modes still holds true. In the case of the IBM 7040/44/90/94 compilers, expressions containing real and double precision terms, or real and complex terms, are accepted.

Problems

Express the following as FORTRAN expressions:

Assume each variable name is one letter in length.

1. $\frac{3 + X}{4Y}$

2. $X + \frac{YZ}{8}$

3. $\frac{X + YZ}{8}$

4. $\frac{A}{B} + \frac{C}{D}$

5. $3AX^2 + BX + C$

6. $\frac{D(V)(R)}{U}$

7. $\frac{4\,(\pi)\,(R^3)}{3}$ (π = 3.14159)

8. A^{BC}

9. $(A^B)^C$

10. $\frac{A + B}{C + \frac{D^2}{E}}$ 3

11. $A\,(X + B\,(X + C))^4$

Logical Expressions

These are expressions constructed from logical variables or from smaller logical expressions. Before we discuss their use in FORTRAN IV it will be well to review briefly the basic concepts governing their use in Boolean algebra.

We are dealing here with the status or condition of a variable rather than its magnitude. The questions we ask are strictly of the true-false type: Is gate G open or closed? Is distance D equal to 6.6 feet or not equal to 6.6 feet? If, in a given circuit, switches A, C and D are open and switches B, E and F are closed, will current flow to light L or will no current flow to light L?

To see how these questions can be set up mathematically and to explore how statements are made about these conditions, we can examine a simple situation:

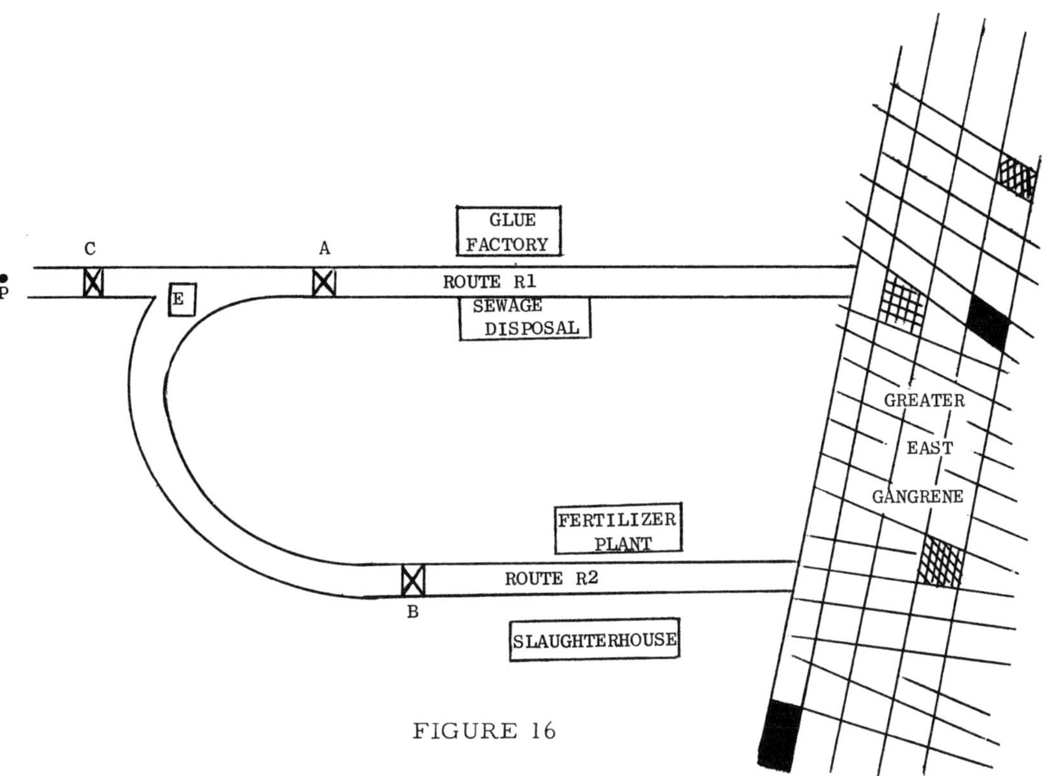

FIGURE 16

East Gangrene Approach Problem

Figure 16 shows two approaches to the metropolis of East Gangrene. Our traveler P, through circumstances beyond his control, finds himself bound for this place. The first logical variable we can assign to this situation is expressed by the statement "he gets to town." Let's represent this by Y. If indeed he does get to town, Y is true (let's call that condition 1); if not, then Y is false (we'll call that 0). The three areas C, A, and B in Figure 16 represent areas where road destruction is going on. At various points in time, conditions at these places are such as to allow passage or prevent passage. We can represent this state of affairs symbolically by setting up a logical variable C, which represents the statement "point C is open to traffic." The same goes for A and B.

Now that our variables are defined, we can say something about how they are related. First, we know immediately that the status of Y depends on the simultaneous conditions at C. If C is false (that is, point C is closed to traffic), P can't get to East Gangrene regardless of what A and B are like. Once he is past C, P can get to town if either A or B (or both) are open. With this in mind, let's place our traveler at location E. Then we can make the statement

$$Y = A \vee B$$

which says "Y depends on A and B in the following way: Y is true if A is true, if B is true, or if both are true." Or, to put it another way, Y can only be false if both A and B are false. In FORTRAN, this type of statement is written

```
Y = A.OR.B
```

To complete the statement of P's predicament, we take note of the fact that C must be true before we can even worry about A or B. This can be expressed as

$$Y = C \wedge (A \vee B)$$

The FORTRAN equivalent is

Y = C.AND. (A.OR.B)

This statement says "Y can only be true if C and A, C and B, or C and B and A are true." When a logical statement is more complex, a systematic investigation of its status can be made by constructing a truth table which shows the prevailing status under all possible combinations. Table V shows the structure of such a table for the East Gangrene Approach Problem.

Table V

Truth Table for the Logical Expression C. AND. (A.OR.B)

IF A IS	AND B IS	THEN THE EXPRESSION (A.OR.B) IS	AND IF C IS	THEN C.AND. (A.OR.B) IS
.TRUE.	.TRUE.	.TRUE.	.TRUE.	.TRUE.
.TRUE.	.TRUE.	.TRUE.	.FALSE.	.FALSE.
.TRUE.	.FALSE.	.TRUE.	.TRUE.	.TRUE.
.TRUE.	.FALSE.	.TRUE.	.FALSE.	.FALSE.
.FALSE.	.TRUE.	.TRUE.	.TRUE.	.TRUE.
.FALSE.	.TRUE.	.TRUE.	.FALSE.	.FALSE.
.FALSE.	.FALSE.	.FALSE.	.TRUE.	.FALSE.
.FALSE.	.FALSE.	.FALSE.	.FALSE.	.FALSE.

There is one more logical operation which is to be discussed and can best be exemplified by the following: Suppose the East Gangrene Planning Commission wisely set things up so that whenever B was open, C was closed and vice versa. This can be expressed as

$$C = \overline{B}$$

which reads "C is not B" (meaning when C is true B is false and vice versa). In FORTRAN this is written

C = .NOT.B

Hence the three logical operators available in FORTRAN are

.AND.

.OR.

.NOT.

The periods must always appear as shown. Expressions constructed with these operators may in turn be combined to form more complex logical expressions. For example, the expression

(A.AND.B).OR.C

may be evaluated from the following truth table:

Table VI

A	B	C	A.AND.B.OR.C
.TRUE.	.TRUE.	.TRUE.	.TRUE.
.TRUE.	.TRUE.	.FALSE.	.TRUE.
.TRUE.	.FALSE.	.TRUE.	.TRUE.
.TRUE.	.FALSE.	.FALSE.	.FALSE.
.FALSE.	.TRUE.	.TRUE.	.TRUE.
.FALSE.	.TRUE.	.FALSE.	.FALSE.
.FALSE.	.FALSE.	.TRUE.	.TRUE.
.FALSE.	.FALSE.	.FALSE.	.FALSE.

Parentheses are used in logical expressions in much the same way as they are in arithmetic expressions. We can illustrate by writing the expression

D. AND. . NOT. (A. AND. B)

Its truth table looks as follows:

Table VII

A	B	A.AND.B	.NOT. (A.AND.B)	D	D.AND. .NOT. (A.AND.B)
.TRUE.	.TRUE.	.TRUE.	.FALSE.	.TRUE.	.FALSE.
.TRUE.	.TRUE.	.TRUE.	.FALSE.	.FALSE.	.FALSE.
.TRUE.	.FALSE.	.FALSE.	.TRUE.	.TRUE.	.TRUE.
.TRUE.	.FALSE.	.FALSE.	.TRUE.	.FALSE.	.FALSE.
.FALSE.	.TRUE.	.FALSE.	.TRUE.	.TRUE.	.TRUE.
.FALSE.	.TRUE.	.FALSE.	.TRUE.	.FALSE.	.FALSE.
.FALSE.	.FALSE.	.FALSE.	.TRUE.	.TRUE.	.TRUE.
.FALSE.	.FALSE.	.FALSE.	.TRUE.	.FALSE.	.FALSE.

If the expression had been written

D. AND. NOT. A. AND. B

then the truth table would look as follows:

Table VIII

A	.NOT.A	B	.NOT.A .AND.B	D	D.AND..NOT. A.AND.B
.True.	.FALSE.	.TRUE.	.FALSE.	.TRUE.	.FALSE
.TRUE.	.FALSE.	.TRUE.	.FALSE.	.FALSE.	.FALSE
.TRUE.	.FALSE.	.FALSE.	.FALSE.	.TRUE.	.FALSE
.TRUE.	.FALSE.	.FALSE.	.FALSE.	.FALSE.	.FALSE
.FALSE.	.TRUE.	.TRUE.	.TRUE.	.TRUE.	.TRUE.
.FALSE.	.TRUE.	.TRUE.	.TRUE.	.FALSE.	.FALSE
.FALSE.	.TRUE.	.FALSE.	.FALSE.	.TRUE.	.FALSE
.FALSE.	.TRUE.	.FALSE.	.FALSE.	.FALSE.	.FALSE

FORTRAN IV also provides means for using arithmetic quantities or expression as parts of larger, logical expressions. This is done by using the relational operators. There are six, as follows:

.LT.	Less than
.LE.	Less than or equal to
.EQ.	Equal to
.NE.	Not equal to
.GE.	Greater than
.GT.	Greater than or equal to

These relational operators are used to connect two real or two integer arithmetic expressions, with the resulting combination becoming a legitimate logical expression. Logical expressions or mixtures of real and integer quantities may not be used with these operators. Let's look at a simple example:

(X. GE. 7. 2)

X is a real variable and 7. 2 is, of course, a real constant. FORTRAN treats the whole expression as follows: If the current magnitude of X happens to be below 7. 2, the entire expression is given a value of . FALSE. Otherwise it would have a value of . TRUE. Listed below are some examples of logical expressions using these operators:

(Y. GT. Z.). AND. W

This says: If real variable Y is greater than real variable Z and logical variable W is . TRUE., then the expression has the value . TRUE.. All other combinations will give the expresssion a value of . FALSE. The same quantities, combined in the expression

Y. GT. (Z. AND. W)

would not be accepted by FORTRAN because the operator . GT. must connect two arithmetic expressions while the . AND. operator can connect only logical expressions. Let's look at a more complex example:

((X ** 2 + 3. * C/D). NE. W). AND. . NOT. G

The truth table for this mess would look as follows:

Table IX

$X^2 + \frac{3C}{D} \neq W$?	G	.NOT.	((X ** 2 + 3.* C/D).NE.W .AND..NOT.G
.TRUE	.TRUE. .TRUE.	.FALSE.	.FALSE.
.TRUE.	.FALSE.	.TRUE.	.TRUE.
.FALSE.	.TRUE.	.FALSE.	.FALSE.
.FALSE.	.FALSE.	.TRUE.	.FALSE.

Since FORTRAN provides means for constructing valid expressions containing arithmetic, logical, and relational operators, an overall priority list must be established for all types. When parentheses are absent, or written a set of parentheses, the order of operations is as follows:

1. Exponentiation (**)
2. Multiplication and Division (* and /)
3. Addition and Subtraction (+ and -)
4. Relational Operations (.LT.,.LE.,.EQ., .NE.,.GE.,.GT.)
5. .NOT.
6. .AND.
7. .OR.

Problems

Correct the illegal logical expressions and construct truth tables for each of them. (Assume mixed modes arithmetic expressions are unacceptable.)

1. I.NE.4.5
2. A.AND..NOT.B
3. C ** 3.LT.J4.OR.B
4. X.OR.(A.AND..NOT.B)
5. X.GE.4.AND.Y ** 2/2..NE.7
6. C.AND..NOT.D.OR.(E.AND.G)
7. A.LT.B.OR.C
8. A.OR.B.AND.C.OR.D
9. J+7.GE.14.AND.B ** 2.5.NE.16.445

Chapter III

Statements Involving Arithmetic and Logical Expressions

Arithmetic Statements

The arithmetic statement is used to instruct FORTRAN to carry out some computations. Its general form is

```
C = B
```

where C is a single variable (of any type) and B is a valid arithmetic expression. The equal sign in FORTRAN is <u>not</u> used in quite the same way as in normal mathematical notation. We can get a more accurate idea if we use the term "IS REPLACED BY" instead of "EQUALS." This denotes a dual type of operation, which can be illustrated with the following example:

```
Y = A*X**2 + B*X + C
```

This statement tells FORTRAN the following:

1. Using the current values of A, B, C and X, do the calculations indicated by the expression to the right of the equals sign.

2. Store the result in a place called Y. Another way of reading this statement would be "Y is replaced by the current value of $AX^2 + BX + C$."

With this kind of meaning given to the equal sign, FORTRAN allows us to do things such as the following:

```
I = I + 1
```

This says, "Add 1 to the current value of I and store the new value in I." As we go on it will be seen how handy this can be.

Arithmetic statements must, like everything else in FORTRAN, conform to some fairly rigid rules. These are as follows:

1. The left side of an arithmetic expression must be in implicit form. Thus the statement

Y - C = A X 2 + B X

is not acceptable. Y must be by itself on the left side.

2. All the members of the right hand expression must be either constants or <u>previously defined</u> variables. The variable on the left side of the equal sign need not be previously defined. In fact, this is often the way computed variables are defined.

3. The right hand expression must be a valid combination of terms but need not be in the same mode as that of the implicit variable. To clarify this, let's use some examples to see how FORTRAN handles mixed modes. In the statement

A = I

A is a real (floating point) variable and I represents some integer expression. I's value will be converted to floating point and stored in A. Conversely in the statement

I = A

I is an integer (fixed point) variable and A represents some floating point expression. Here the value of A will be truncated to the nearest integer, which will then be stored in I. Let's examine this further: Say we have

X = 9/5

FORTRAN will divide the integer 9 by the integer 5, truncate the answer, convert it to floating point, thus storing a floating point 1 (or 1.) in X. If we had written

X = 9./5.

we would, of course, have gotten the entire quotient (or 1.8). Similarly, the statement I = 9/5 will result in the integer 1 being placed in I; and the statement I = 9./5. will result in floating point division, truncation to 1, conversion to an integer, and storage in I.

Since double precision numbers are subject to the same rules as single precision real numbers, they can be used in real expressions and arithmetic statements. A look at several statements involving single and double precision expressions will illustrate how these are treated. Let's assume that X and Y are previously defined single precision variables and W and Z are previously defined double precision variables.

1. W = 3.E2 *X + Y

This statement will cause FORTRAN to multiply X by the single precision value of 300, add Y to the result, and store the sum as a double precision number in W. In this case, the second word of memory reserved for W will have all zeroes in it since the computations were performed using single precision arithmetic.

2. Y = 3. D2 * X + W

In this case, the computations are performed using double precision arithmetic. Then the most significant portion of the result is stored as a single precision value in the single word Y.

Statements involving complex variables and constants may not contain any other types, on either side of the = sign. Thus, if B and C are previously defined complex variables, an example of a valid statement would be

C = (3.0, 4.7) * B

which reads "multiply the current value of the complex variable B by the quantity 3 + 4.7i and store the result in the address reserved for the complex variable C."

Logical Statements

As in the case of arithmetic statements these are used to define variables and/or to instruct FORTRAN to do computations. The left-hand side of the equal sign must be a single logical variable and the right-hand side must be a legitimate logical expression of any degree of complexity. Statements like

C = D.AND..NOT.(A.AND.B)

and

B = Y.NE.4.*X**3/Z.AND.W.GT.7.*X

are perfectly valid logical statements as long as all the variables to the right of the equal sign have been previously defined, so that they have current values. To reinforce this concept, let's set up a truth table for the second statement given above:

Table X

Truth Table for the Statement B = Y.NE.4.X**3/Z.AND.W.GT.7.*X

Y	W	B
$Y \neq \frac{4X^3}{Z}$	W>7X	.TRUE.
$Y \neq \frac{4X^3}{Z}$	$W \not> 7X$	.FALSE.
$Y = \frac{4X^3}{Z}$	W>7X	.FALSE.
$Y = \frac{4X^3}{Z}$	$W \not> 7X$	.FALSE.

Y, X, Z and W must have been defined previously, either by some arithmetic statements, type declaration statements, or as a result of having been read in as input.

Problems

1. Express the following as FORTRAN statements or expressions. Assume each variable name is one letter long.

a) $\frac{3 + X}{4Y}$

b) $X + \frac{YZ}{8}$

c) $\frac{X + YZ}{8}$

d) $V = \frac{4 (\pi) (R^3)}{3}$ (π = 3.14159)

e) $D = A^{BC}$

f) $D = (A^B)^C$

g) $\frac{A}{B} + \frac{C}{D}$

h) $AX^2 + BX + C/E$

i) $R = \frac{D\,(V)\,(R)}{U}$

j) $\frac{A + B}{C + \left(\frac{D}{E}\right)^2} = F - 4$

k) $A\,(X + B\,(X + C))^4$

2. Indicate the values of Y and I in the following statements:

a)	Y = 2.* X **2/4. + 3. 0 *X/(X + 2.0)	X = 4.0
b)	Y = 3.* X/2. * 4.	X = 6.0
c)	I = M** 2 * N ** 2	M = 3, N = 4
d)	I = (M * N)**2	M = 3, N = 4
e)	Y = X*(3. * X - 2) / (X ** 2 + 4.)	X = 6.0
f)	I =I - 4	I = 10
g)	I = 4 K - 8 *K*J	K = 2, J = 3
h)	Y = (X + 3.)* 4.** 2	X = 2.0
i)	I = J *J/J **2	J = 6

3. A medical researcher measures the flow of blood through a vein over a known period of time. If T is the time in seconds, W is the number of grams of blood collected and D is the blood's density in grams/cc, write a FORTRAN IV statement for V, the blood flow in cc per minute.

4. Find the value of logical variable A:

a)	A = I.GE.J	I = 4, J = 3
b)	A = C.NE.D	C = 6, 0, D = 6
c)	A = .NOT.(B.AND.C)	B = .TRUE., C = .TRUE.
d)	A = (B.OR.C) .AND..NOT(C.AND.D)	B = .TRUE. C = .FALSE. D = .TRUE.

5. If X and Y are real variables and A is a logical variable, write a statement to carry out the following:
Place the value .TRUE. in A if neither X^2 nor $\frac{Y^3}{5}$ exceed a magnitude of 4.

6. A man intent on committing suicide throws himself off the top of a building, giving himself an initial rate of fall of V1 feet per second. If the gravitational constant is taken as 32.174 feet/second/second, and this nut is assumed to be in free fall, write a FORTRAN statement which expresses the distance he has fallen, D, in terms of his initial velocity (V0) and the time elapsed (T) since his jump.

7. A frequently used equation for calculating the convective heat transfer coefficient H looks as follows:

$$H = 0.023\left(\frac{DV}{U}\right)^{0.8}\left(\frac{UC}{B}\right)^{0.4}$$

where each of the names is one letter long. Write a FORTRAN expression for this calculation.

8. The change in nuclear reactor density is given as a function of reactor material properties and temperature by the expression

$$\frac{-6B^2M^2}{k}\left(\frac{d1}{d2}\right)^3 \frac{\alpha}{[1+\alpha(T2-T1)]^4}$$

Write a legitimate FORTRAN expression, naming variables accordingly.

9. The total amount of money in a bank account is given by the expression P + P x R x T. Express this relationship in a FORTRAN expression.

10. If a manager has N subordinates reporting directly to him in groups as well as individually, an expression can be written which gives the total number of different interactions that are possible between manager and subordinates. This takes the form

$$N\,(2^N/2 + N - 1)$$

Express this in FORTRAN.

The Use of Functions in Arithmetic Statements

In many instances it becomes necessary for a certain type of computation (or set of computations) to be performed at several different stages during the execution of a program. Or, several programs require the same type of computation as part of their respective sequences. To avoid having to work out and write the sequence every time it is used, programming languages provide means whereby the sequence is written only once by the programmer. His and/or other programs may then use it by including it in their programs and calling on it whenever it is necessary (closed subroutines) or by using some type of cue statement which will cause the assembler or compiler to insert the proper instructions automatically (open subroutines). Many standard mathematical functions fall into this category of oft-repeated calculations.

FORTRAN IV provides a number of commonly used mathematical functions which can be used directly in arithmetic expressions and statements. These functions have standard names which, when used, will cause the compiler to reference prearranged set of instructions, which, when executed, will compute the desired function. Such a function, for example, might be used as follows:

Y = SIN (X)

The compiler would take the current value of X and use it in a preset series of instructions (routine or subroutine) after which the sine of X would be stored in Y. The sequence of instructions is built into the permanent FORTRAN library and can be used any number of times in a given program. This is called a library (or closed) function. The quantity in parentheses (called the argument) need not be restricted to a variable but may, in fact, be an expression. For example,

Y + SIN (X** 2 - 26. * Z)

is perfectly valid as long as X and Z have been defined previously. A table of available functions is given below. Y and X are used for illustrative purposes and represent arguments. The name shown in the leftmost column is the preassigned names for calling the function. The use of commas indicates the presence of more than one argument. The expression with which these functions are used must be in the proper mode (single precision, double precision or complex, as appropriate) and must adhere to the other requirements for legality of the expression.

There are an additional set of functions which are used the same way as those previously listed. Their construction in the compiler, however, is different. In this case, a reference to a given function produces no referral to an already prepared sequence of instructions. Instead the compiler produces a specific set of instructions right then and there. Thus, every time this type of function is called, the compiler generates another, identical set of instructions. This group of functions is called built in (or open) functions.

Table XI

Mathematical Functions Available in FORTAN IV

A. Single Precision

X, Y and Z are Real Quantities

FORTRAN Statement	Mathematical Equivalent
Y = EXP(X)	$Y = e^{X}$
Y = ALOG(X)	$Y = \text{Log}_e X$
Y = ALOG10(X)[(A)]	$Y = \text{Log}_{10} X$
Y = ATAN (X)	$Y = \text{Tan}^{-1}(X$, Y in radians
Y = ATAN2(X, Z)[(B)]	$Y = \text{Tan}^{-1}(X/Z)$, Y in radians
Y = SIN(X)	Y = Sine X, X in radians
Y = COS(X)	Y = Cosine X, X in radians
Y = TANH(X)[(B)]	Y = Tanh X
Y = SQRT(X)	$Y = \sqrt{X}$
Y = ARSIN(X)[(C)]	$Y = \text{Sin}^{-1} X$, X in radians
Y = ARCOS(X)[(C)]	$Y = \text{Cos}^{-1} X$, X in radians
Y = CUBERTF(X)[(D)]	$Y = \sqrt[3]{X}$
Y = POWRF(X, Z)[(D)]	$Y = X^{Z}$

(A) Not available on the CDC 3200/3400/3600

(B) Not available for the IBM 360, 1401, 1440, 1460, UNIVAC III, CDC 3200

(C) Available only on the IBM 7040/7044

(D) Available only on the CDC 3600/3400

Note: Function names in CDC 3600/3400 FORTRAN are as above except that an F is added (e.g. EXPF(X), SINF(X), etc).

Table XI (continued)

Mathematical Functions Available in FORTRAN IV

B. Double Precision *

W, B, and D are Double Precision Quantities

FORTRAN Statement	Mathematical Equivalent
W = DEXP (B)	$W = e^{B}$
W = DLOG (B)	$W = \text{Log}_e B$
W = DLOG10 (B)$^{(E)}$	$W = \text{Log}_{10} B$
W = DATAN (B)	$W = \text{Tan}^{-1} B$, W in radians
W = DATAN2 (B, D)$^{(E)}$	$W = \text{Tan}^{-1}(B/D)$, W in radians
W = DSIN (B)	W = Sine B, B in radians
W = DCOS (B)	W = Cosine B, B in radians
W = DSQRT (B)	$W = \sqrt{B}$
W = DCUBRT (B) $^{(F)}$	$W = \sqrt[3]{B}$

* Not available on IBM 1401, 1440, 1460, UNIVAC III, RCA 3301, CDC 3200

(E) Not available on CDC 3600/3400/3200

(F) Available only on CDC 3600/3400

Table XI (continued)

Mathematical Functions Available in FORTRAN IV

C. Complex Numbers *

G and H are Complex Quantities

FORTRAN Statement	Mathematical Equivalent
H = CEXP (G)	$H = e^{G}$
H = CLOG (G)	$H = \text{Log}_e\, G$
H = CSIN (G)	H = Sine G
H = CCOS (G)	H = Cosine G
H = CSQRT (G)	$H = \sqrt{G}$
H = CATAN (G) (A)	$H = \text{Tan}^{-1}\, G$
H = CDEXP (G) (B)	$H = e^{G}$ where H and G are double precision
H = CDLOG (G) (B)	$H = \text{Log}_e\, G$
H = CDLG10 (G) (B)	$H = \text{Log}_{10}\, G$
H = CDSIN (G) (B)	H = Sine G
H = CDCOS (G) (B)	H = Cosine G
H = CDSQRT (G) (B)	H = G
H = CABS (G) (B)	If G = A + Bi, $H = \lvert \sqrt{A^2 + B^2} \rvert$

* Not available on IBM 1401, 1440, 1460, UNIVAC III, RCA 3301, CDC 3200

(A) Available only on CDC 3600/3400

(B) Available only on IBM 360

TABLE XII
Open Functions Available in FORTRAN IV
A. Real and Integer Quantities*
Y and X are Single Precision, I and J are Integers

Sample FORTRAN Statement	Purpose
Y = ABS (X)	Places absolute value of X in Y
I = IABS (J) or I = XABS (J)[(A)]	Places absolute value of J in I
Y = AINT (X) or Y = INTF (X)[(A)]	Truncates X to largest integer value and stores in Y in floating point mode
I = INT (X) or I = IFIX (X)	Truncates X to largest integer value and stores in I integer mode
Y = AMOD (X,Z) or Y = MODF (X,Z)[(A)]	Computes and stores in Y the value X - [X/Z] *Z where [X/Z] is the integral part of (X/Z)
I = MOD (J,K) or Y = MODF (J,K)[(A)]	Computes and stores in I the value J - [J/K] *K where [J/K] is the integral part of (J/K)
Y = AMAX0 (I,J,K, etc.) or Y = MAX0F (I,J,K, etc.)[(A)]	The maximum value in the list is chosen and stored as a floating point number in Y
Y = AMAX1 (X,Z, etc.) or Y = MAX1F (X,Z, etc.)[(A)]	The maximum value in the list is chosen and stored as a floating point number in Y
I = MAX0 (J,K, etc.) or I = XMAX0F (J,K, etc.)[(A)]	The maximum value in the list is chosen and stored as an integer in I
I = MAX1 (X,Y,Z, etc.) or I = XMAX1F (X,Y,Z, etc.)[(A)]	The maximum value in the list is chosen and stored as an integer in I
Y = AMIN0 (I,J,K, etc.) or Y = MIN0F (I,J,K, etc.)[(A)]	The minimum value in the list is chosen and stored as a floating point number in Y
Y = AMIN1 (X,Z, etc.) or Y = MIN1F (X,Z, etc.)[(A)]	The minimum value in the list is chosen and stored as a floating point number in Y
I = MIN0 (J,K, etc.) or I = XMIN0F (J,K, etc.)[(A)]	The minimum value in the list is chosen and stored as an integer in I
I = MIN1 (X,Y,Z, etc.) or I = XMIN1F (X,Y,Z, etc.)[(A)]	The minimum value in the list is chosen and stored as an integer in I
Y = FLOAT (I) or FLOATF (I)[(A)]	The I is stored as a floating point number in Y
Y = SIGN (X)	The sign of X is transferred to Y
I = ISIGN (J)	The sign of J is transferred to I
Y = DIM (X,Z) or Y = DIMF (X,Z)[(A)]	The quantity X minus X or X minus Z, whichever is greater, is stored as a positive number in Y
I = IDIM (J,K) or I = XDIMF (J,K)[(A)]	The quantity J minus J or J minus K whichever is greater, is stored as a positive number in I
Y = SIGN (X,Z)[(B)] or Y = SIGNF (X,Z)[(A)]	A number having the magnitude of X and the sign of Z is stored as a real quantity in Y
I = ISIGN (J,K)[(B)] or I = XSIGNF (J,K)[(A)]	An integer having J's magnitude and K's sign is stored in I
Additional Functions Available in CDC 3600/3400 FORTRAN	
I = ITOJ (J,K)	$I = J^K$
Y = XTOI (X,I)	$Y = X^I$
Y = RANF (I)	A random number is generated and placed in Y

(A) CDC 3600/3400 form

(B) Available only on RCA 3301, CDC 3600/3400, IBM 360, RCA SPECTRA 70.

Table XII (continued)

Open Functions Available in FORTRAN IV

B. Double Precision Numbers*

W, B, and D are Double Precision Quantities

Sample FORTRAN Statement	Purpose
Y = SNGL (B)	Places the significant portion of B in the single word Y.
W = DBLE (Y)	Y is placed in W in double precision form.
W = DABS (B)	Places absolute value of B in W.
I = IDINT (B)	Truncates B and places the integer value in I.
W = DMAX1 (B, D, etc)	The largest algebraic value of the list is placed in W.
W = DMIN1 (B, D, etc)	The smallest algebraic value of the list is placed in W.
W = DSIGN (B)	The sign of B is transferred to W.

* Available in IBM 360, RCA SPECTRA 70, IBM 7040/7044/7090/7094, PHILCO 2000.

Table XII (continued)

Open Functions Available in FORTRAN IV

C. Complex Numbers *

G and H are Complex Quantities of the form E + Fi

Sample FORTRAN Statement	Purpose
Y = REAL (G)	The real portion of G is placed in Y.
Y = AIMAG (G)	The imaginary portion of G is placed in Y.
H = CMPLX (X, Y)	The complex quantity X + Yi is **found** and placed in H.
G = DCMPLX (W, B)(A)	The complex, double precision quantity W + Bi is found and placed in G
H = CONJG (G) or H = CCONT (G)(B)	If G contains E + Fi, H will contain E - Fi.
H = DCONJG (H)(A)	Same as CONJG except that the argume involved are double precision.
Y = CANG (G)(C)	The angle associated with the complex quantity G is stored, in radians, in Y.

* Available only on IBM 360, RCA SPECTRA 70, IBM 7040/7044/7090/7094, CDC 3400/3600, PHILCO 2000.

(A) Available only on IBM 360.

(B) CDC 3400/3600 form

(C) Available only on CDC 3400/3600

Means by which additional functions may be constructed and included will be discussed under the section on subprograms.

Problems

1. If A and B are the sides of a right triangle, write a program to find the hypotenuse. Store the answer in a place called HYPTNS.

2. Write a program to find the roots of the equation

$$AX^2 + BX + C = O$$

place the roots in Y1 and Y2.

3. A coroner examining a murder victim finds that the bullet entered the victim's body at an angle of BETA degrees from the horizontal and at a height of HIGH feet from the ground. Based on the assumption that the murderer lay on the ground while he shot the victim, write a program to calculate the distance at which the victim was shot.

4. A fancy doctor receives calls from four hypochondriac patients, each of whom wants the doctor to visit. The doctor knows that these cranks will pay him 11, 12, 13 and 14 dollars respectively, for visits which he knows will last T1, T2, T3 and T4 hours, respectively. However, legitimate calls restrict the doctor to no more than one hypochondriac. Write a program that will tell the doctor what the highest rate (dollars per hour) will be for a single hypochondriac visit.

Subscripted Variables

Arrays (or matrices) are sequences of values (elements) for a variable listed in some given order. In ordinary mathematical notation, the location of any single element in an array is defined by a subscript. Thus if ten values of X are listed or used in sequence, X_7 is the seventh one. If the listing is simply sequential the array is one-dimensional. A two dimensional array has two ways of defining its elements. Suppose, for example, the density of a liquid were to be listed as a quantity varying with temperature and pressure. We could represent the listing as follows (T is temperature, P is pressure and D is density).

	T_1	T_2	T_3	T_4 $\cdots$	T_N
P_1	D_{11}	D_{12}	D_{13}	D_{14} $\cdots$	D_{1N}
P_2	D_{21}	D_{22}	D_{23}	D_{24} $\cdots$	D_{2N}
P_3	D_{31}	D_{32}	D_{33}	D_{34} $\cdots$	D_{3N}
P_4	D_{41}	D_{42}	D_{43}	D_{44} $\cdots$	D_{4N}
$\vdots$	$\vdots$	$\vdots$	$\vdots$	$\vdots$ $\cdots$	$\vdots$
P_M	D_{M1}	D_{M2}	D_{M3}	D_{M4} $\cdots$	D_{MN}

The pressures are the rows, temperatures are the columns and the density values are the elements. Each element is uniquely located by a double subscript denoting its row number and column number, in that order. The whole array can then be given a single name, such as D.

FORTRAN usually handles up to three subscripts (three dimensional arrays). (Exceptions include the IBM 360, which allows seven, and the SDS 9300,which has no limit.) Subscripts must be integers and are placed inside parentheses following the variable name. These subscripts are restricted to certain forms. If, for example, X is some subscripted variable, M and N are integer constants (unsigned) and I is an unsigned integer variable, then the allowable types of subscripts are as follows:

Table XIII

Allowable Forms for Variable Subscripts

Form	Written in FORTRAN as
X_I	X (I)
X_M	X (M)
X_{I+M}	X (I + M)
X_{I-M}	X (I - M)
$X_{M(I)}$	X (M*I)
$X_{M(I)+N}$	X (M*I + N)
$X_{M(I)-N}$	X (M*I-N)

FORTRAN is quite particular about the forms used for subscripting array variables. The order of the components in a subscript must be followed, as well as the structure; this is illustrated in Table XIV.

Table XIV

Legal Form	Unacceptable Form
X (M + 3)	X (3 + M)
X (M - 7)	X (7 - M)
X (3 * M)	X (M * 3)
X (3 * M + 6)	X (6 + 3 * M)

Several additional rules must be followed strictly when it comes to subscripting:

1) Subscripts must always be integers or integer expressions.

2) All subscripts are to be unsigned.

3) Each variable which is subscripted must have the size of its array specified elsewhere in the program, in a place preceding the first appearance of the variable with

subscripts. This is done via a DIMENSION statement as discussed later.

4) The elements of any one array must all be in the same mode.

5) Calculated subscripts must be such that their value will never be zero or negative. Thus, for example, in the element X (J - 3), the value of J must always be 4 or greater.

6) Subscripts in a multidimensional array are separated by commas.

Problems

Select the invalid subscripts and correct them:

1) X (I, J, K)
2) BETA (3 - J)
3) FLOW (J + 3, J - 3)
4) MASS (3)
5) HALF (4 * M)
6) DNSTY (3 *K, S* L - 4. 2)
7) SPEED (3*J, I, 2* L)
8) LOAD (3 - 4 * L)
9) LOAD (3, + 4 *L)
10) Y (I + 3, A, 3*K - 4)

Representation of Arrays in Memory

The storage of multidimensional lists in a computer's memory is controlled by the FORTRAN compiler and is designed to take maximum advantage of the particular processors's internal logical structure. As a result, the FORTRAN compiler for a given machine uses one of two basic storage sequences.

The system used with most types of computers is one in which the first subscript varies most rapidly, followed by the second, and so on. Thus, in the case of a two dimensional array called B having M rows and N columns, the lowest address assigned to the array will contain $B_{1,1,}$ the next address will contain $B_{2,1}$ and the sequence will be

$$B_{11}, B_{21}, B_{31}, \ldots, B_{M1}, B_{12}, B_{22}, B_{32}, \ldots, B_{M2}, \ldots, B_{1N}, B_{2N}, B_{3N}, \ldots, B_{MN}$$

Similarly, a three dimensional array having dimensions of L by M by N would be stored in the sequence

$$B_{111}, B_{211}, B_{311}, \ldots, B_{L11}, B_{121}, B_{221}, \ldots, B_{L21}, \ldots,$$
$$B_{1M1}, B_{2M1}, \ldots, B_{LM1}, \ldots, B_{11N}, B_{21N}, \ldots, B_{LMN}$$

or, expressed in FORTRAN

B (1, 1, 1), B (2, 1, 1), etc.

Note that an element in an array is still referred to as it would be in regular mathematical notation. That is, the subscript gives the row number, column number, block number, etc., even though FORTRAN does not store the elements in that order. As an example, let's suppose we have the two dimensional array called X shown below:

	Column 1	Column 2	Column 3	Column 4
Row 1	17	2	7	40
Row 2	4	23	9	46
Row 3	96	61	18	52
Row 4	29	44	66	3
Row 5	15	5	36	27

These will be stored in the order 17, 4, 96, 29, 15, 2, 23, 61, 44, 5, etc. However, X_{23} will still be 9, X_{52} will be 5, X_{14} will be 40, and so on. This is called forward storage.

For certain types of computers (including the IBM 1401, 1410, 1440, 1460) it is more convenient for FORTRAN to store arrays in a fashion which is the reverse of that described above. The subscripting remains the same insofar as the programmer is concerned. It is this internal operation of the compiler which is different. In such a computer, FORTRAN would store the array given in the previous section in the following order: 27, 3, 52, 46, 40, 36, 66, 18, 9, 7, 5, etc. Note that X_{23} is still 9, X_{52} is still 5, and so on. (This is known as reverse storage.)

Problems

1. There are 15 numbers stored in a one-dimensional array called X. Assuming the array has been dimensioned previously write a FORTRAN statement which will serve to calculate the sum of every third element, beginning with the second one. This sum should be stored in a place called SUM.

2. Shown below is a three-dimensional array called STRONG in which the tensile strength of an alloy is given for varying compositions: (The remaining component is iron.)
If the row variable is % Cr (10, 15, 20, 25) the column variable is % Ni (5, 6, 7) and the block variable is % Co (1, 2, 3).

a) State the values of

STRONG (4, 2, 2)

STRONG (1, 2, 1)

STRONG (2, 3, 3)

STRONG (4, 3, 2)

b) Show the sequence in which the values would be stored in a computer using forward storage.

% Cr	% Ni	% Co	Strength	% Cr	% Ni	% Co	Strength
10	5	1	12	20	5	1	22
10	5	2	14	20	5	2	29
10	5	3	16	20	5	3	31
10	6	1	13	20	6	1	34
10	6	2	15	20	6	2	36
10	6	3	17	20	6	3	37
10	7	1	18	20	7	1	41
10	7	2	25	20	7	2	43
10	7	3	40	20	7	3	44
15	5	1	20	25	5	1	32
15	5	2	23	25	5	2	35
15	5	3	26	25	5	3	39
15	6	1	21	25	6	1	45
15	6	2	24	25	6	2	46
15	6	3	27	25	6	3	48
15	7	1	28	25	7	1	47
15	7	2	33	25	7	2	49
15	7	3	38	25	7	3	50

Chapter IV

Control Statements

Thus far we have spoken about programs which are composed of statements to be executed in direct and unvarying sequence. It is, however, often desirable or necessary to alter the sequence of execution, depending on some input and/or computed conditions. Several statements in FORTRAN make use of the computer's decision-making ability, thus allowing the programmer to set up alternate paths under a variety of conditions. Statement numbers, discussed in the first chapter, serve as signposts which allow these control statements to be used effectively.

The GO TO Statement

The simplest FORTRAN statement for altering the sequence of execution is the GO TO statement, which transfers control to another section of the program. This statement appears in the form

```
GO TO n
```

where n is some statement number. Suppose for example, we measured blood pressure before and after treatment on a group of patients and we wanted to determine the percent change in pressure. If PRESS1 and PRESS2 are the before and after readings, respectively and DELTP is the percent change, we could write a program as follows: (Operations not yet covered are shown in block form)

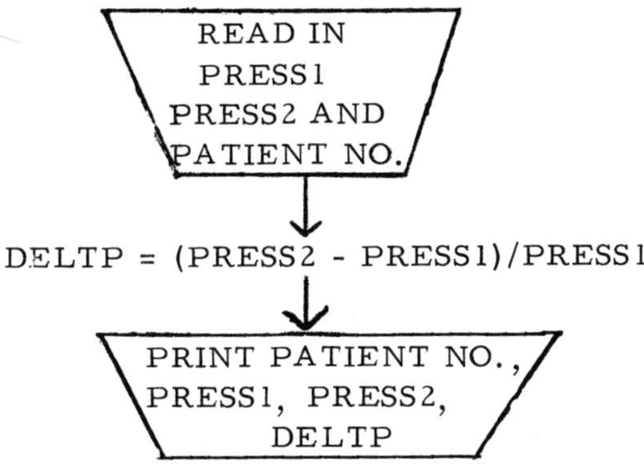

This is fine except that it will handle only one patient. For each additional patient it would be necessary to reload the program. We can make use of the GO TO statement by numbering the first of the "read in" statements and transferring control to it immediately after printing the data for the previous patient. This might look as follows:

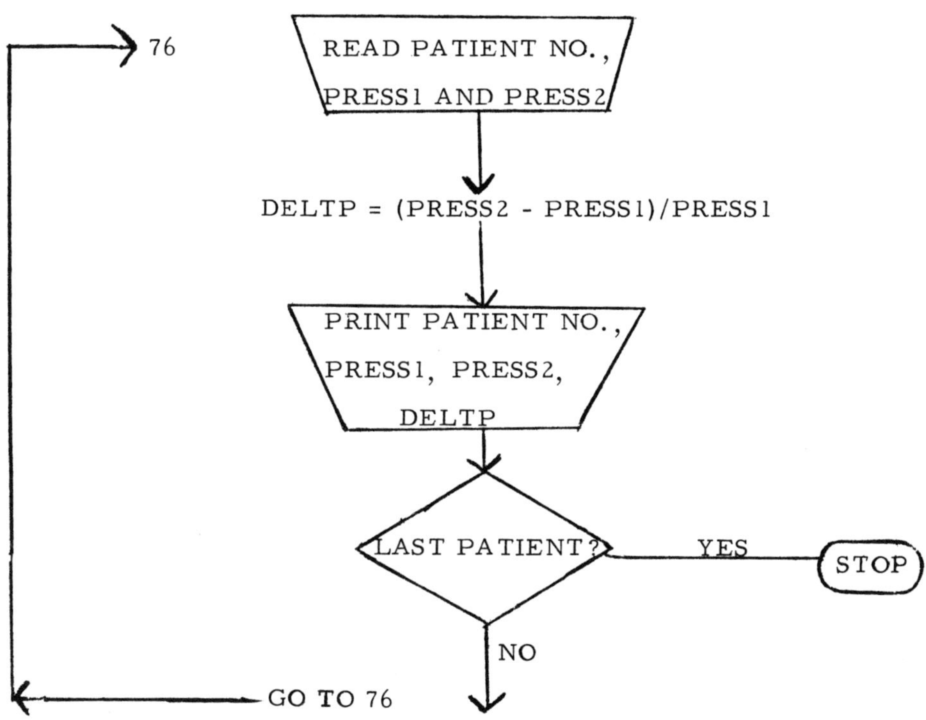

Thus the program will go on reading, computing and printing until it runs out of patients. (No pun intended).

Computed GO TO Statement

This statement is used in the form

$$\text{GO TO } (n_1, n_2, n_3, \text{etc.}), \text{ J}$$

where n_1, n_2, etc., are statement numbers and J is a non-subscripted integer variable. The computed GO TO provides a means for selecting one of several alternate instruction sequences depending on conditions during a given run. The value of J, let's say, is computed at some point in the program and then dictates, at some later point, the path which is to be followed. For example, we can consider a program segment as shown below:

```
J = N ** 2 - 1      where N is some integer variable
next statement      read into the program
next statement
      .
      .
      .
      .
GO TO (17, 5, 21, 100, 3, 2), J
next statement
      etc.
```

This will cause the program to transfer control to the first statement in the list (no. 17) if J = 1, second statement (no. 5) if J = 2, and so on. Caution must be used to avoid the following: If J turns out to be zero or less, or a number greater than the number of statements listed in the parentheses, the program will stop running and cause an error message to be printed. Thus, in the example given above, J must never exceed a value of 6, since there are only 6 alternate statements listed. Don't forget the comma between the closing parenthesis and the integer variable.

The Assigned GO TO Statement

This statement provides a way to preset one of several directions which a program may follow. The general form is

GO TO L, (n_1, n_2, n_3, etc.)

In this case the program transfers to the statement which has a number equal to the current value of L, L must always be one of the numbers listed in the parentheses. Otherwise the program will stop running and an error message will be printed. Values of L are set by an ASSIGN statement which appears as follows:

ASSIGN M to L

where M is a statement number which matches one of those appearing in the list of the assigned GO TO statement. Naturally, the ASSIGN statement must appear in the program somewhere prior to the GO TO. Thus, if we have a program segment which includes

```
      ASSIGN 18 TO L
      next statement
      next statement
         etc.
GO TO L, (17, 21, 18, 6, 101, 49)
```

control will be transferred to statement no. 18. Watch the comma in front of the parentheses.

IF Statements

The IF statement combines the functions of a GO TO statement and a test on the value of an expression. As such it finds wide use in determining which of several alternate paths a program should follow.

Arithmetic IF Statement

Before explaining this statement it should be noted that FORTRAN IV accepts this statement only to maintain consistency with previous FORTRAN compilers. The more generalized logical IF statement will be emphasized.

The IF statement allows the FORTRAN programmer to set up decision criteria which will dictate the selection of alternate paths. An example will clarify:

$$\text{IF (X) } n_1, n_2, n_3$$

This says "If the value of X is less than 0, go to statement number n_1 and continue from there. If X is zero, go to statement number n_2. If X is larger than zero go to statement number n_3 and continue from there." X may be any legitimate <u>arithmetic</u> expression except those containing complex terms and n_1, n_2 and n_3 are statement numbers appearing in the program (all three numbers need not be different). As an example of the use of the arithmetic IF statement, suppose a medical investigator has a program in which he wishes to determine the accumulation of cadmium in a group of paint factory workers. He measures the cadmium concentration in milligrams per milliliter at some initial time, calling this CON1 and also the concentration after some standard time interval T. The second concentration is called CON2. The rate of accumulation is called ACCUM. If this rate exceeds some critical level, CRIT, the investigator wants a count (NCRIT) of these. The program segment might look something like this:

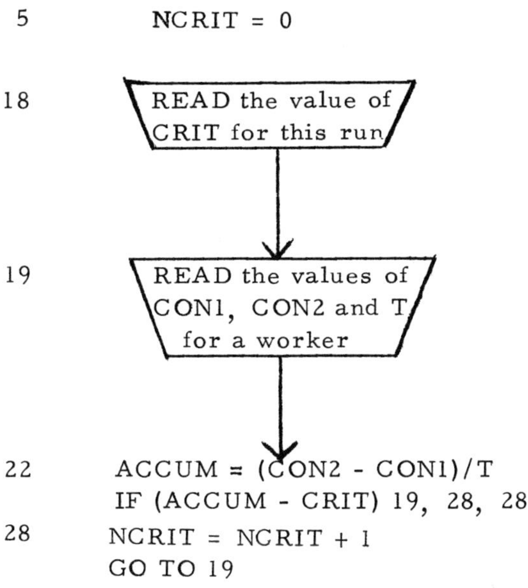

So: After having read in the critical value which is to be used for this run, the data for a worker are read in. The accumulation is computed and then compared to the critical value. If it is less than the critical value, the program goes on to read the data for another worker. If the accumulation is equal to or greater than the critical value, the count of critical accumulations is increased by 1. Notice that the integer variable NCRIT was defined early in the program by writing an arithmetic statement setting the value to zero at some point prior to the introduction of data. This process is called <u>initialization.</u>

The Logical IF Statement

The general form for this statement is

```
IF (E) S
```

E represents any legitimate logical expression and S represents any executable FORTRAN statement except another IF or a DO statement (which we'll cover next). The logical IF works as follows: If the logical expression E is true, the program will execute statement S. If expression E is false, the program will disregard statement S and proceed to the next statement. Here are some examples:

```
IF (A.AND.B) X = - X
```

If logical variables A and B both are .TRUE. at some given point in time, change the sign of real variable X. If not, skip this statement.

```
IF (N.GE.20) GO TO 9
```

If integer variable N reaches or exceeds a value of 20, go to statement number 9. Otherwise continue in regular sequence.

```
IF (D) GO TO L, (17, 21, 9)
```

If logical variable D is .TRUE., execute the assigned GO TO as dictated by the value of L. Otherwise proceed in normal sequence.

The FORTRAN compilers for the CDC 3600/3400/3200 computing systems provide an additional version of the logical IF statement in which two transfer choices are given. An example is shown below:

IF (X. LE. 17.* Y) 46, 52

If the logical expression enclosed in parentheses is . TRUE. (i. e., if X is less than or equal to 17Y), the next statement to be executed will be no. 46. If X is greater than 17Y, then the expression if false and the program will transfer instead to statement no. 52.

Problems

Use logical IF statement where IF statements are required.

1. Suppose we have four real variables in storage, called A, B, C and D. Write a program which checks the values of A, B, C and D. If all four values are less than 30, go to statement 19. If only two variables (any two) are less than 30, go to statement 18. All other combinations of values are to be sent to statement 17.

2. We have a one-dimensional array of values in storage called X. There are 29 values in this array (they can be called X (1) to X (29)). Write a program to add the X's together until the sum reaches a number equal to or greater than 1604. When this happens, go to statement number 14. As part of the program, find and store the number (subscript) to the last X value used in a place called XLAST. If all 29 add up to less than 1604, go to statement 301.

3. In the following program segment, X = 14.0, Y = 12.0, Z = 20.0, W = 6.0, R = 8.0. For these values, determine the statement which will be executed immediately following the IF statement:

```
T = (Y** 2 + Z) / ((W + R) / X)
ASSIGN 17 TO K
S = T/4.
IF((S - 1.).NE. (2*Z)) GO TO K, (21, 44, 106,
                  17, 9, 51)
```

4. There is an array of 107 single precision floating point numbers in storage called Y. Find the odd numbers and place them in ascending order in array X. Find the even numbers and place them in descending order in array Z. Store the number of odd numbers in NODD and the even count in NEVEN.

5. An array M contains 5281 integer values. Write a program segment to search the array. If a value is evenly divisible by 17, it is to be added to SUM17; if evenly divisible by 9, it is to be added to SUM9; if evenly divisible by both 6 and 8 it is to be subtracted from SUM68. All other values are to be added to SUMGEN.

The DO Statement

This is possibly the most powerful single statement in FORTRAN since it causes the compiler to generate a relatively large number of actual machine instructions. The DO statement allows the controlled repetition of a given sequence of instructions. Its usefulness becomes most apparent when applied to subscripted variables, which can be handled quite easily in groups or entire arrays, as dictated by the programmer.

As an example let us suppose we have a one-dimensional array in storage called X, with 197 elements in the array (that is to say X (1) through X (197)). We wish to find the sum of the squared values of X. Without using the DO statement our program loop might look as follows:

	Statement	Remarks
	SUM = 0.0	An area called SUM is initialized.
	I = 1	A counter called I is set to 1.
10	SUM = SUM + X (I) ** 2	Add the square of the current X element to the sum of squares.
	IF (I. GE. 197) GO TO 25	If we've squared all 197 elements, go to statement 25.
	I = I + 1	If not, add one to the counter and continue squaring.
	GO TO 10	
25	Some other statement	

This same program segment, when written with a DO statement, looks like this:

	Statement	Remarks
	SUM = 0.0	We still initialize SUM
	DO 10 I = 1, 197, 1	
10	SUM = SUM + X (I) ** 2	
25	Some other statement	

The DO statement here says "Execute the instructions immediately following this statement UP TO AND INCLUDING statement number 10. Start with subscript number 1, and repeat the sequence until you reach subscript number 197, increasing the subscript by one each time." Suppose we wanted every other element in the array squared and summed instead of using all the elements. We would then write

```
         SUM = 0.0
         DO 10 I = 1, 197, 2
10       SUM = SUM + X (I) ** 2
25       Some other statement
```

This would take X_1, square it, add it to SUM, then do the same to X_3, X_5, X_7, etc., till it processed X_{197}. Let's say we wanted only the even-numbered subscripts processed. We could write

```
         SUM = 0.0
         DO 10 I = 2, 197, 2
10       SUM = SUM + X (I) ** 2
25       Some other statement
```

Now the first element to be used would be X_2, then X_4, etc. When the program got to X_{196}, processed it, and added 2 to the subscript, the upper limit (197 in this example) would be exceeded. Consequently X_{196} would be the last element processed. We could just as easily have written

```
DO 10 I = 2, 196, 2
```

However, in many cases it will turn out that the upper limit on the subscript number is not known in advance, but instead is a variable which has previously been computed or was read in as part of the data (input). This makes the automatic limiting feature very useful. Now that we have looked at the example we can set up the general form for the DO statement:

$$\text{DO N I} = K_1, K_2, K_3$$

N is the number of the last statement included in the cycle (or DO loop), thus specifying the RANGE of the DO loop. I is the INDEX of the DO loops, since it is the indicator which will be changing as the program cycles and recycles. K_1 is the initial value at which the index is to be set, K_2 is the upper limit, or test value for the index, and K_3 is the number by which the index is to be incremented as the loop is executed and re-executed. Certain rules must be obeyed with respect to the construction of a DO statement:

1) N must be a statement number matching the one at the desired end of the loop.
2) I must be a fixed point (integer) variable.
3) K_1, K_2, and K_3 must be unsigned integer constants or non-subscripted integer variables which have been defined prior to the entrance to the DO loop. Most FORTRAN compilers require that K_1, K_2, and K_3, whether constants or variables, always exceed zero. (An exception is found in CDC 3600/3400/3200 FORTRAN IV, which permits values of zero as below for K_1 and K_2 when they are variables.)
4) If K_3 is omitted, it is understood to be 1; in such cases, the comma preceding K_3 must also be omitted.

5) If K_2 should exceed K_3, the DO loop will not be executed in most cases. IBM 360 FORTRAN is an exception in that if it encounters a DO loop in which K_3 is less than K_2, it will allow that loop to be executed once.

6) Once the loop has been executed the appropriate number of times, the index is undefined and its value is not available for subsequent use.

7) With the exception of the CDC 3600/3400/3200, FORTRAN IV does not permit the changing of K_1, K_2, or K_3 values in the middle of a DO loop. In the exceptional cases, K_2 and K_3 may be changed. Thus the program segment

```
      DO 26 I = 1, 16
      Y (I) = 3. * X (I) - 4.
   26 I = I + 2
```

would be illegal.

The use of the index need not restrict itself to a subscript. It may, in fact, be used as any other fixed point variable within the range of the DO loop. This can be illustrated with the following program segment:

```
      L = 24
      K = 0
      DO 17 M = 2, L, 3
      K = K + 2
   17 Y (M) = (J(M) + K) / M
```

This would cause the following sequence:

a) An integer L is defined, having a value of 24.

b) An integer K is defined, having an initial value of zero.

c) Starting with the second element is an array called J, every third element is used in calculating a corresponding Y, which is stored in an array of Y's. Each time this is done, the value of K is increased by 2:

$$Y_2 = \frac{J_2 + 2}{2}$$

$$Y_5 = \frac{J_5 + 4}{5}$$

$$Y_8 = \frac{J_8 + 6}{8}$$

$$Y_{11} = \frac{J_{11} + 8}{11}$$, and so on, until we reach

$$Y_{23} = \frac{J_{23} + 16}{23}$$

d) After this last cycle, the program would try using X_{26}, which is above the limit set by the previously defined value of L; consequently the program would climb out of the loop and proceed with whatever statement follows statement number 17.

Nesting of DO Loops

It is perfectly legal to use DO loops within other DO loops as long as certain conditions are met:

1) The inner loop must be totally contained within the range of the outer loop. For example:

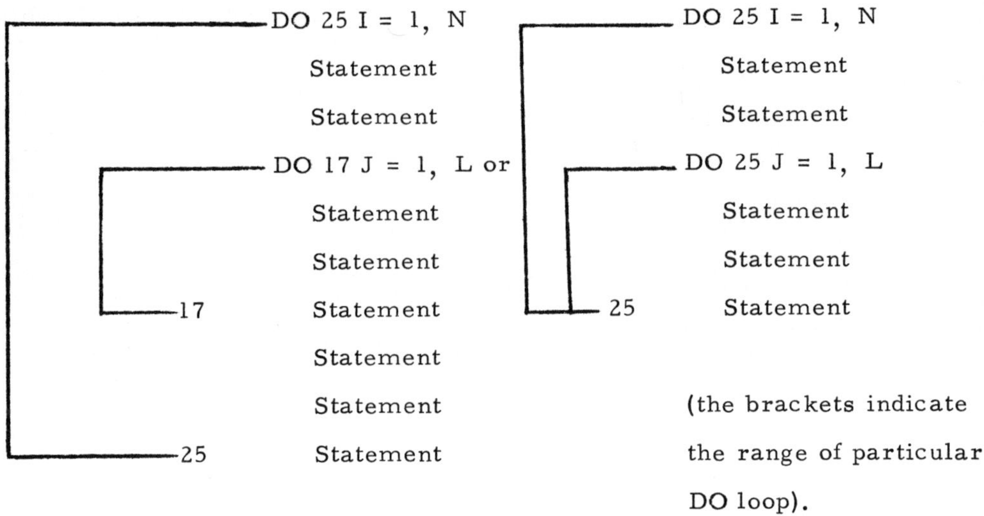

are both legal. The arrangement

```
       DO 15 I = 1, N
          Statement
          Statement
       DO 17 K = 1, L
          Statement
          Statement
15        Statement
17        Statement
```

is not acceptable.

2) Control may at any time be transferred from somewhere inside

a DO loop to somewhere outside it, but not vice versa. Thus the following schematics represent legal transfers:

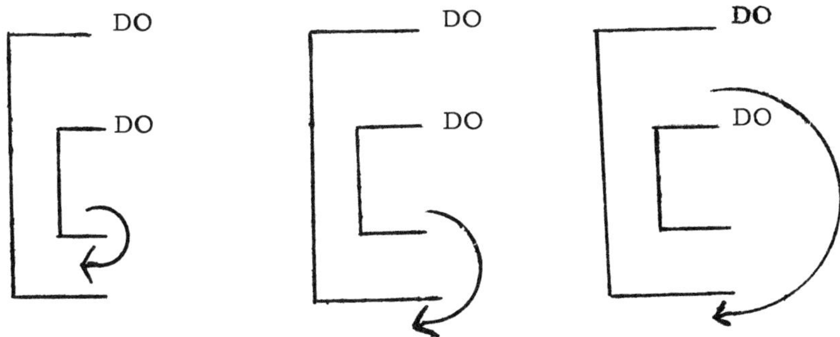

The next three are all illegal:

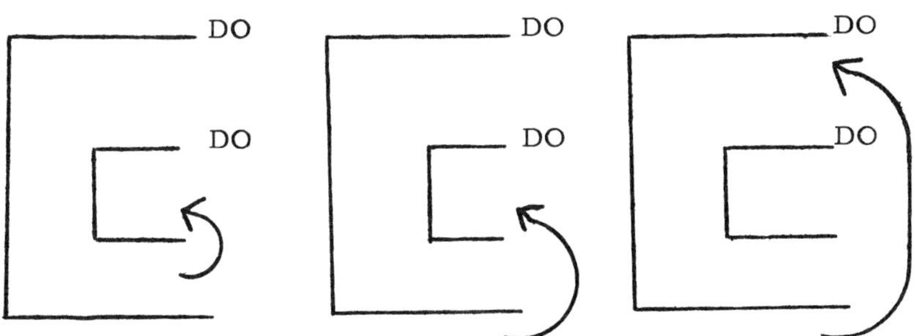

There is one exception. In a nested set of DO loops, a transfer may occur from the innermost loop and then back into it as long as none of the loop's parameters (I, K_1, K_2, K_3) are changed in the process.

3) After the program has exited from a DO loop the same index names may be re-used, but they must be re-initialized. If a DO loop is constructed such that control is transferred out of the loop's range, the index (or indices) will retain their values at the time of transfer.

4) The index of one DO loop may be used by another within that nest. Thus, for example,

```
        DO 30 I = 1, 24
        DO 26 J = I, 33
26      Y (J) = Y (J) + I
30      X (I) = X (I) - I**2
```

5) A loop cannot end with a GO TO or arithmetic IF statement. If the loop is ended with a logical IF, the following happens:

If the logical expression is false, the DO loop is executed again (reiterated). If the logical expression is true, the statement referred to at the end of the IF is executed and <u>then</u> the loop is reiterated. If the statement at the end of the IF is a control transfer statement, however, control is transferred. Let's look at examples:

```
25      DO 31 K = 1, 20
        X (K) = 3. * Y (K) - Z (K)** 2
31      IF (Z(K).GE. 3* Y) GO TO 44
```

In this example, if $Z_i \geqslant 3\,Y$, the program would execute statement 44. If $Z_i < 3\,Y$ and K had not yet reached 20, the program would go back to statement 25. Now, in the example

```
25      DO 31 I = 1, 20
        X (I) = 3. * Y (I) - Z (I) ** 2
31      IF (Z(I).GE. 3 *Y) X(I) = 7. * Y (I) - Z(I)** 2
```

In this case, if $Z_i < 3\,Y(I)$, then X_i is calculated as $3Y - Z^2$ and the program goes back to statement number 25 without executing the $X_i = 7Y_i - Z^2$ step.

There are limits to how many DO loops may be nested. However, these are usually large enough to preclude concern (e.g. 25 on the IBM 360, 50 on the CDC 3600).

The CONTINUE Statement

This is not an executable statement. Instead, it is a dummy statement used by the compiler to get around the restriction defined in rule 6) above. As such, CONTINUE is used as the last statement in a DO loop where the programmer wants a transfer address for an IF or GO TO statement which is intended to begin another iteration of the DO loop. For example:

```
19      DO 27 I = 1, 13, 2
        Y (I) = Z (I) + SIN (X(I))
        IF (X.GT. 3.14159/2.) GO TO 31
27      CONTINUE
```

Thus the dummy statement provides a convenient reference for the end of the DO loop's range.

The PAUSE Statement

This is written as

```
PAUSE   N
```

where N is an integer constant which may also be blank. When the computer encounters the PAUSE statement, it stops processing and displays the number N on some visual output device or console. If no number is specified, zeroes are usually produced. This allows the programmer to set landmarks in a program so that manual action may be taken, if desired. Pushing the START button after a PAUSE will allow the computer to resume processing where it left off.

The IBM 360 also provides capability for displaying messages as well as numbers as part of PAUSE statements. Thus one may write

```
PAUSE 'LET IT HAPPEN'
```

when 'LET IT HAPPEN' is any legitimate literal constant.

The STOP Statement

This terminates the execution of a program. In those computing systems where the FORTRAN compiler is part of a large overall supervisory program system, the STOP statement causes execution to cease and control to revert to the supervisory program.

Some FORTRAN compilers allow a second version of the STOP statement:

```
STOP N
```

Here again, the computer stops and the integer N is displayed on some output device or the processor's console. Restarting the processor turns control over to the supervising program. The IBM 360,

RCA SPECTRA 70, PHILCO 2000, and CDC 3600/3400/3200 have this capability.

The END Statement

This must be the physically last statement in a program. As such it is a signal to the compiler to stop compiling.

Problems

1. Write a program to calculate the number of ways of making change for a dollar. Store the result in NWAYS.

2. Write a program for calculating X ! and store the value in XFACT.

3. Write a program to compute the following:

$$Y = \sum_{i=1}^{N} \frac{1}{\sqrt{X_i}}$$

If any value of X is zero, make $\frac{1}{\sqrt{X_i}}$ zero. Store the number of zero values in a place called NZERO.

4. A radiologist measures counts on an isotope sample every 20 minutes for 5 minutes (5 minutes of counting, 15 minutes of waiting, 5 minutes of counting, etc.). The background count value in counts per minute is stored in NBCKGD. Write a program to calculate net counts per minute (raw counts/minute minus background) for N readings, and average counts per minute. Also, store the maximum counts per minute in a place called CTMAX.

5. A medical investiagator wants to generate a table of penicillin injection volumes in cc, together with corresponding strength in USP

units. Write a program which will generate a two-dimensional array in which the first column is the volume in cc from 1, by halves to 50, and the second column contains the corresponding strength where strength = 150 times the volume to the 3/2 power.

6. Write a program which finds all three digit numbers such that when the number is added to a transposition of those digits, the result is another of those digits. For example:

$$\begin{array}{rr} & 495 \\ + & \underline{459} \\ & 954 \end{array}$$

(Thus 495 and 459 would each count as such a number.) Store the count of such numbers in MANY. (Assume that the memory for all necessary arrays has already been allocated.)

Chapter V

Input and Output Statements

Up to this point we've considered only internal statements and have assumed that the input got into the machine somehow and that by some means, the output was transformed into some readable form. We shall now consider the basic input/output statements which handle these functions.

Peripheral Unit Designation

Before information can be transmitted to or from a processor, the proper circuits must be activated so that the operation proceeds properly. This is especially critical when several input and output devices are attached to a processor. Each program must indicate which of these units is to supply input and which is to receive results. In the case of more complex processing procedures, where such transmission may involve more than one input or output device, means must be provided for the completely unambiguous selection of the appropriate device each time a piece of information is transmitted.

In most earlier versions of FORTRAN, separate types of statements were provided for use with specific types of peripheral devices. If the programmer wanted the information from a punched card to be read into the machine he would, at the desired point in his program, use a statement like

```
READ 14 X, Y
```

This statement would be interpreted by FORTRAN roughly as follows: "Since the statement doesn't say where to read from, I'll assume that the information to be read is on a punched card. I am to read two pieces of information and store them in memory, calling the two storage places X and Y. A statement numbered 14, included somewhere in the program, will tell me where on the card the two pieces of information are located and what forms they are in (whether numbers or letters, etc.)." If the input information were stored on magnetic tape, the "read" statement would take the form

READ INPUT TAPE 4 X, Y

In this situation the machine would be directed to read two pieces of information from the tape unit whose dial is set at # 4. Similarly, output devices were referenced by specific statements like

PRINT 14 X, Y or

PUNCH 14 X, Y or

WRITE OUTPUT TAPE 3, 14, X, Y

With the introduction of newer computing systems and a greater variety of input/output devices, it became necessary to write very flexible programs which would control the processing of data more automatically and efficiently. One of the features built into these supervisory programs is the ability to keep track of which peripheral units are being used for a given processing job. This is usually done by designing a supervisory program which will accept a certain maximum number of peripheral units as being attached to a given computing system. The program maintains a table in memory in which each peripheral unit is assigned to a specific attachment number, called a logical unit number. These assignments may be changed from job to job, depending on the particular needs. Furthermore, with this arrangement, the same supervisory program will serve a number of installations, each having the same central processor but a different peripheral constellation. To see how this works, let us say that a particular system allows as many as five (5) peripheral devices to be attached. Thus, in its assignment table, the supervisory program has assignment slots for logical units 1 - 5. For a given job, unit 1 might be the card reader, unit 2 the printer, unit 3 the output card punch, unit 4 a tape drive whose dial is set to # 2 and unit 5 a second tape drive whose dial is set to # 7. Such assignments may be specified by each user. If no assignments are made, the supervisory program assumes that the most recent assignments still hold.

Computers equipped with such supervisory program systems are, in general, also equipped with FORTRAN compilers which operate under control of these systems. Consequently, the input/output statements in FORTRAN IV refer to logical units rather than actual physical devices. This information is passed on to the supervisory program which selects the proper device as dictated by its assignment table.

With this concept of logical units in mind, we can proceed to the input/output statements themselves.

The READ Statement

This statement takes the general form

READ (M, N) list

In this statement, M is an integer which defines the unit from which the input is to be read, N is the number of a FORMAT statement in which is given the form of the input data and "list" specifies the number of pieces of data to be read and the order in which they appear in the input. Thus, the statement

READ(5, 16)X, Y, J,

indicates to FORTRAN that three (3) pieces of data are to be brought into the processor. The first two are floating point numbers and are to be assigned locations X and Y, respectively. The third, a fixed point quantity, is to be stored in J. Number of digits in each quantity, number of decimal places, in X and Y, etc., are given in statement no. 16. The unit number, 5 in this sample statement, is transmitted by FORTRAN to the supervisory program which consults its unit assignment table to determine which physical unit is to be referenced. In many supervisory systems, the number 5 is reserved for input use only. Depending on the particular circumstances, unit # 5 may be a card reader, a magnetic tape drive, or other input device. In any event, when such a reservation is made, it becomes impossible to produce output on that unit and it is referred to as the <u>system input unit.</u> For our purpose we shall assume that the system input unit is a card reader unless otherwise noted.

The simplest type of list in a READ statement is one in which each entry represents a single individual value, such as in the example

READ (5, 19) X, DNSE, Y, J2, AMAX, TIME, N

In this case, the READ statement sets up instructions which will read seven values from a card as defined in a FORMAT statement (number 19). Any additional quantities on that card will be ignored. Conversely, if a single card contains less than seven quantities, a sufficient number of cards will be read until seven quantities have been found and stored as specified in the READ statement. In any event, this type of READ statement will allow only one set of values for the specified variables to be read.

Reading Arrays

The READ instruction can also be written so as to introduce entire arrays of data into the computer. This is done by setting up a type of DO loop. For example, the statement

```
READ (5, 21) (X(I), I = 1, 10)
```

will set up a loop which will read 10 values from a card (or cards) as directed in FORMAT statement 21, and store these values in X_1 thru X_{10}. This takes the place of the more tedious form

```
READ (5, 21) X (1), X (2), X(3), X(4), X(5), X(6), X(7), X(8), X(9), X(10)
```

Let's explore this implied DO loop a little more. We have seen thus far that the list in a READ statement may contain two types of entries separated by commas: The single value, which may or may not carry a subscript, and the multivalued array, enclosed by parentheses, which can be read in using an implied DO loop. FORTRAN accepts all combinations and degrees of complexity in READ statements. It is therefore important that the workings of these lists be understood. Let's look at an example that is a little more involved:

READ (5, 6) (C(I), D(I, J), I = 1, 5), X

This would set up machine instructions such that the following values would be read and stored before the program proceeded to the next instruction:

C(1), D(1, J), C(2), D(2, J), C(3), D(3, J), C(4), D(4, J), C(5), D(5, J), X.

Note that this is quite different from the statement.

READ (5, 6) (C(I), I = 1, 5), (D(I, J), I = 1, 5), X

In this case, the first five values read in will be stored as C values, the next five as D values, and finally, the single value of X. Complete two dimensional arrays are handled similarly. The statement

READ (5, 10) ((A (I, J), J = 1, 3), I = 1, 4)

will transmit data in the order

A(1, 1), A(1, 2), A(1, 3), A(2, 1), A(2, 2), A(2, 3), A(3, 1), A(3, 2),
A(3, 3), A(4, 1), A(4, 2), A(4, 3).

If we had written

READ (5, 10) ((A (I, J), I = 1, 4), J = 1, 3)

the order of transmission would have been

A(1, 1), A(2, 1), A(3, 1), A(4, 1), A(1, 2), A(2, 2), A(3, 2), A(4, 2),
A(1, 3), A(2, 3), A(3, 3), A(4, 3).

We should note at this point that elements of a list in a READ statement must be unsigned and implicit. Subscripts in a list must follow the rules stated previously for subscripting.

Now let's set up one more complex example for a READ:

```
READ (5, 26) B(6), S, ((R(I, J), I = 1, 5, 2), S(J), J = 1, 4)
```

The quantities read off the card (or cards, as directed by FORMAT statement number 26) would be transmitted and interpreted to be the following list of values, in the order given:

B(6), X, R(1, 1), R(3, 1), R(5, 1), S(1), R(1, 2), R(3, 2), R(5, 2),
S(2), R(1, 3), R(3, 3), R(5, 3), S(3), R(1, 4), R(3, 4), R(5, 4), S(4).

One more thing; if the length of an array of values is defined in a DIMENSION statement (more about this later) we can use a shorthand notation in our READ statement. For example, the statement

```
READ (5, 7) B
```

will read in the entire array called B. If the size of B was not defined in a previous DIMENSION statement, then only the initial element of the B array will be read in. A note of caution: With one-dimensional arrays, everything is fine. With two dimensional matrices, however, this can only be used if the elements are listed columnwise on the cards, since that's how the machine will store them. Suppose we have defined an array called W as having 2 rows and 3 columns, and we write the statement

READ (5, 9) W

This is the same as if we had written

READ (5, 9) ((W(I, J), I = 1. 3), J = 1, 2)

giving us transmission and storage in the order

W(1, 1), W(2, 1), W(3, 1), W(1, 2), W(2, 2), W(3, 2).

Note also that the following type of statement is perfectly legal:

READ (5, 11) N, (A(I), I = 1, N)

FORTRAN will use the N it has just read in to regulate the implied DO loop.

A number of systems are equipped to accept a third form of the READ statement:

READ N, list

In this statement, only the number of the appropriate FORMAT statement (N) is given; the input unit is not specified but, rather, is understood to be the system input unit. (The IBM 1401, 1410, 1440, 1460, and the Control Data 3200 will not handle this form.)

When an input unit number is specified, the designation may be in the form of a variable whose value is determined in some statement prior to the READ instruction. To illustrate, it is possible to write the sequence

```
M = 4
READ (M, 17) X, Y
```

resulting in the transmission of two values into the processor from logical unit # 4 in the form specified in FORMAT statement number 17.

The WRITE Statement

The rules set down for READ statements apply to the WRITE statement, which takes the general form

WRITE (M, N) list   or   WRITE N, list

where M, N and "list" have the same meanings as in the READ statements. Again, as in the READ statement, the length of the list determines the extent of the writing. It should be remembered of course, that each variable in such a list must be defined in some prior statement. In many supervisory systems, the number 6 is reserved for designating the system output unit. This may be a printer, magnetic tape drive, or other device. Similarly, on those computing systems equipped with an output punch, the number 7 is reserved for this unit. Again, for illustrative purposes, we shall assume that unit # 6 always specifies a printer.

It is also possible to specify a WRITE statement without giving a list. Thus

WRITE (6, 21)

tells the compiler that the programmer wishes to produce output on the printer and that the actual information to be written is contained in FORMAT statement number 21 and was generated internally by the processor.

Transmission of Binary Information

Since information is stored and manipulated in a processor as strings of binary bits (combinations of 1's and 0's), the compiler must include provisions for translating into binary form when non-binary information is read in, and reconverting into readable and understandable form when output is to be written. These conversions are, relatively speaking, fairly slow and, if large amounts of data are involved, may be quite time-consuming. Of course, this is unavoidable in most cases. However, in those instances where a program is producing output which is intermediate data for a given problem or project and is to be examined only by a subsequent part of the program or by some other program, conversion can be avoided. Such output may be transmitted to a peripheral device directly in binary form. For example, a program designed to prepare and print payroll checks might read the necessary information about each employee (pay rate, hours worked , standard deductions, etc.) from a reel of tape prepared during the run for the previous pay period. Appropriate modifications, additions and deletions would be read in from punched cards and merged with the data from tape to produce the checks and generate a new (updated) payroll tape containing all of the latest information, to be used for the next run. Such a tape would likely be produced in binary form. This not only saves time but allows more data to be stored per foot of tape, thus, in many cases, precluding the necessity of using multiple reels for a given job.

Binary form is specified in FORTRAN IV as follows:

```
READ (M) list     or
WRITE (M) list
```

where M and "list" have their usual meanings. Again, as in other READ/WRITE statements, the length of the list determines the amount of information transmitted. When the peripheral medium being used is magnetic tape, the output produced by a binary WRITE statement is treated by the processor as a single unit. Consequently, it is essential that the lists in corresponding READ and WRITE statements be identical in length and form. Going back to our payroll example, if we were to produce output on tape with the statement

```
WRITE (3) X, Y, Z, J, K
```

and wished to read only the first four pieces of data from the tape, the list would still have to enumerate five pieces, three real values followed by two integers. The program would then ignore the last value read in.

FORMAT specifications as to size and type of data, usually followed by the compiler during the data conversion processes, are not needed here.

Table XV summarizes the READ/WRITE forms available on various computers.

Table XV

Summary of READ/WRITE Statement Characteristics

Types	Not Available On
READ (M, N) list WRITE (M, N) list	————
READ (M) list WRITE (M) list	————
READ N list WRITE N list	IBM 1401, 1410, 1440, 1460 CDC 3200

The FORMAT Statement

This is a non-executable statement used in conjunction with READ and WRITE statements. For READ statements it supplies information as to which columns on a card contain which variables, what form they are in and how large they are. For WRITE statements, the FORMAT statement gives directions as to where on the paper (or punched card) each output value should be placed as well as the size of the variable and in what form it should be printed. Since FORMAT statements are non-executable, they may be placed anywhere in a program. Each FORMAT statement must have a statement number so that proper reference can be made in the appropriate READ and WRITE statement. The general form is

$$\text{FORMAT } (S_1, S_2, S_3, \ldots\ldots S_N)$$

where each of the S's represents a separate format specification. We'll start with a simple example and work our way up.

Fixed Point Form (I-Conversion)

Figure 17 shows two statements which might constitute the input section of a program. It is seen that we're telling the machine to read eight values from a card and that these values represent M (1) through M (8) in that order and should be stored as such. Notice that there are eight format specifications in the FORMAT statement, each having an I followed by a number. This type of specification indicates that the value is to be treated as an integer having a length specified by the number. Thus, I6 is a six digit integer, etc. Now it must be realized that when a program is written, the instructions and specifications are set up to accommodate the largest anticipated values. Thus, if there is an I5 specification in a FORMAT statement, it does not necessarily mean that every value for that variable must be five digits long. It means, rather, that the program will transmit no more than five digits for that variable. Four of these five digits or, for that matter, all five, may be zeros or blanks. As in ordinary mathematical notation, numbers are always written right-adjusted. For example, the number 23 written in a five digit field would be

00023 or bbb23 (b's represent blanks).

This is also the way they would be punched on a card. Thus, for Figure 17, the machine will store the first six digits as an integer in M (1), the next six digits as an integer in M (2), etc., till eight values are read and stored.

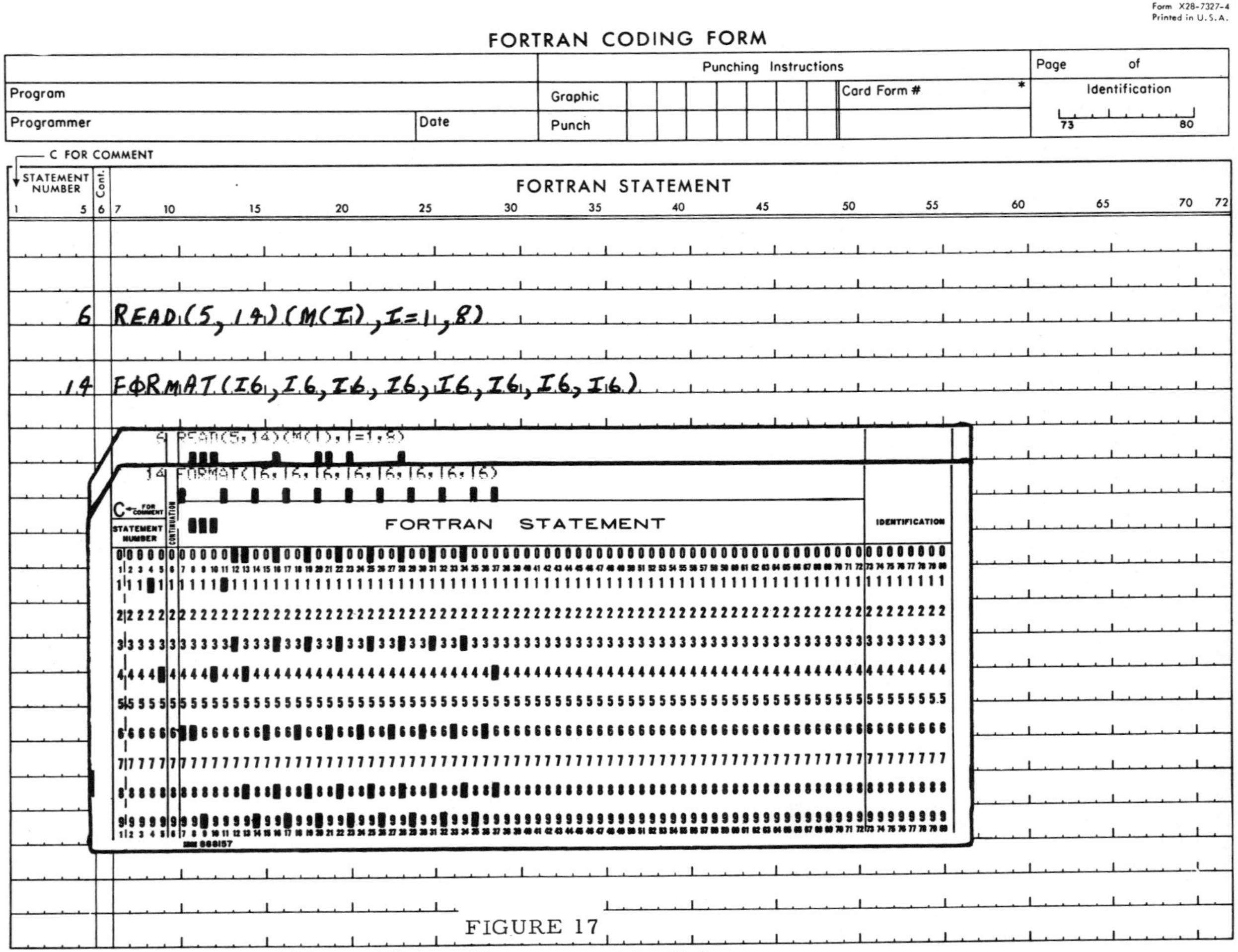

Form X28-7327-4
Printed in U.S.A.
FORTRAN CODING FORM
Program
Programmer
Date
Punching Instructions
Graphic
Punch
Card Form # *
Page of
Identification
73 80
C FOR COMMENT
STATEMENT NUMBER
Cont.
FORTRAN STATEMENT
1 5 6 7 10 15 20 25 30 35 40 45 50 55 60 65 70 72
6 READ(5,14)(M(I),I=1,8)
14 FØRMAT(I6,I6,I6,I6,I6,I6,I6,I6)
6 READ(5,14)(M(I),I=1,8)
14 FORMAT(I6,I6,I6,I6,I6,I6,I6,I6)
C FOR COMMENT
STATEMENT NUMBER
CONTINUATION
FORTRAN STATEMENT
IDENTIFICATION
IBM 888157

FIGURE 17

* A standard card form, IBM electro 888157, is available for punching source statements from this form.

Now that we've seen how this statement works, we can introduce a shorthand form, which applies when several successive specifications are identical. The statement

FORMAT (8I6)

will accomplish the same purpose as the statement given in Figure 17. One more thing. If an I-specification contains a smaller number than the number of significant digits in a stored value, the excess leftmost digits will be lost. A value of 45997 read or written with an I4 specification will produce 5997.

Now we can get to the other types of format specifications.

Floating Point Form (F-Conversion)

Floating point, or F-Conversion takes the general form

Fw.d

where w specifies the number of digits involved and d defines how many of these w digits belong to the right of the decimal point. Let's use as an example the format specification

F6.2

If the computer is given this specification when reading in information it will transmit six digits of information to memory and store them as a floating point number having two decimal places. Thus a number punched as 629741 will be stored in a form equivalent to 6297.41. Hence the decimal point need not be punched on the card but is, in fact, implied in the format specification. If the actual decimal points are punched on the cards they will supercede the format specification. This same specification used with a WRITE statement will cause the information stored in the location designated in the list to be converted and produced as output in the specified form. Thus, the decimal point is correctly inserted and printed. To provide for this, w, the field size, must include 3 extra digits for decimal point and sign.

Given below is a list showing how the number -72.69647 will be printed using various floating point (F-conversion) format specifications:

Format Specification	Internal (Stored) Value	Number Produced
F11.6	-72.69647	-72.696470
F11.5	-72.69647	-72.69647
F10.6	-72.69647	-72.696470
F10.5	-72.69647	-72.69647
F9.6	-72.69647	-72.696470
F9.5	-72.69647	-72.69647
F8.5	-72.69647	72.69647
F7.5	-72.69647	2.69647
F7.4	-72.69647	72.6964
F6.4	-72.69647	2.6964

Exponential Form (E-Conversion)

Exponential or E-conversion takes the general form

EW.d

This results in the transmission of W digits containing a decimal number, the exponent field showing the power of 10 to which the number is to be raised to obtain the correct magnitude, and appropriate signs for the number (mantissa) and its exponent. Any of the allowable exponent forms previously discussed under "constants" can be used as input, as long as the proper number of digits are specified in the FORMAT statement. When an E-conversion is specified for an output (WRITE) statement, care must be exercised to provide enough digits to take care of signs, etc. Suppose we have a number in storage whose true value is 67.49126. FORTRAN, when instructed to write this number in exponential form, will try to produce the following:

+0.6749126E+02

This requires 14 digits, or <u>seven more than the number of decimal places.</u> Hence, the correct format specification would be

E 14.7

Listed below are several forms for the number -266.5048 when given various E-conversion specifications:

Format Specification	Interval (Stored) Value	Number Produced
E14.7	-266.5048	-0.2665048Eb03
E13.6	-266.5048	-0.266504Eb03
E12.6	-266.5048	-0.26650Eb03

Double Precision Form (D-Conversion)

A specification of the type

DW.d

will store input data as double precision information or produce output in exponential form. The number of significant digits available with this specification depend, of course, on the memory structure of the particular processor. These limits are the same as given in Table IV for double precision constants. Thus, for example, a value of -1716.41469776 written with a format specification of D18.9 will produce

.1716414697760Db04

causing a loss of sign. A specification of D19.8 would be more appropriate, giving

-0.171641469776Db04

If a specification is given which exceeds the limits for that particular processor/compiler, the maximum number of digits will be produced.

Formatting Complex Data

Since the real and imaginary components of a complex variable are stored as two distinct pieces of information, their transmission requires two separate format specifications (F-, E-, or D- may be used). For example, the quantity 3.72 + 14.4i, written in FORTRAN as

(3.72, 14.4) would require a format specification of the type (F5.2, F5.1) to produce the entire value. If such a specification were used in conjunction with a WRITE statement, the comma and parentheses will not appear in the output.

Octal Form (O-Conversion)

Many FORTRAN IV compilers include provisions for transmitting data as octal quantities (to the base 8). Use for this form is limited and, in fact, this feature is not present in several recent compilers. We'll describe it here for reference purposes.

The general form is Ow where w represents the number of digits to be transmitted. Limits on w for various computing systems are shown in Table XVI. (Extra large w's may be used to provide blank spaces to the left of numbers when they are being written.

Table XVI

Maximum Field Length for O-Conversion

Computer Type	Maximum No. of Digits
IBM 7040/44/90/94, Philco 2000	12
CDC 3600/3400, UNIVAC III	16
RCA 3301	10
CDC 3200	8 for integers 16 for real values

The General Numerical Format Specification (G-Conversion)

An interesting type of format specification is provided by the IBM 360 FORTRAN compiler. The G-specification is a multipurpose form which will determine the form of transmitted data whether those data are real, integer, complex, or logical. The basic form for this specification is

Gw.p

where w is the total length of the field (including allowances for sign, exponent, and leading zero), and p represents the number of significant digits (not the number of decimals) to be transmitted.

When used with real data, a G-specification causes FORTRAN IV to set aside four of the w digits for an exponent (such as E+02). Having done this, the compiler checks the magnitude of the value to be formatted. If this value is between 0.1 and 10^p, the reserved four-digit exponent field is left blank. Otherwise it is filled in as necessary with E ± nn or D±nn, depending on the length of the real data. As an example, suppose we had the value 18.63749 in storage and printed it with a number of different G-specifications. This is summarized below.

Stored Value	Format Specification	Result
18.63749	G12.7	1 8 . 6 3 7 4 9 b b b b
	G12.5	b b 1 8 . 6 3 7 b b b b
	G11.6	1 8 . 6 3 7 4 b b b b

Note that when an insufficient number of significant digits are specified, the number is truncated rather than rounded off.

When used with integers, the p portion of the specification need not be included. If it happens to be there it will be ignored. Suppose for example, that a FORMAT specification were used with two WRITE statements as follows:

```
       WRITE (6, 17) X
       WRITE (6, 17) N
17     FORMAT (G13.6)
```

If the stored value of X is 17.3427 and N is an integer whose current value is 261, the first WRITE statement will produce

bb17.3427bbbb

and the second WRITE statement will produce

bbbbbbbbbb261

The format specification G13 would produce the same output as shown above.

Scale Factors

FORTRAN allows the programmer to change the order of magnitude of input and output data in a format specification. This is done by using the scale factor or P-Conversion. With input it is used together with F-Conversion fields. With output it can be used in conjunction with either E or F conversions. In any case the general form is

nP

where n is an integer which represents the power of 10 by which the number is to be multiplied before it is stored as input or written as output. Let's illustrate this:

Suppose we had a number in storage whose value was 52.7043. To write it out as such we could use the specification

FORMAT (F9.4)

If we modify the specification to read

FORMAT (2PF9.4)

FORTRAN will print 5270.4300. If we had written

FORMAT (-1PF9.4)

the number bbb5.2704 would be printed. When used with D or E-Conversion numbers, the scale factor changes both the mantissa and the exponent. Thus, if we have a number stored as -57.464 and give a FORMAT specification of

FORMAT (E12.5)

we would produce -0.57464Eb02. A change in format to

FORMAT (1PE12.5)

would produce -5.74640Eb01. The additional decimal figure is brought from storage if available and thus may serve to add another significant digit to the accuracy. By using scale factors it also becomes possible to deal with quantities outside of the range allowed by FORTRAN by doing the calculations on scaled data and then rescaling just prior to printout.

When scale factors are used with input data, the data must be in real form (not E or D). For example, a value punched on a card as 674.31 will be stored internally as such when read in with a FORMAT specification of F6.2. The quantity as stored in memory for various scaled specifications is shown below:

FORMAT	Value Stored
F6.2	674.31
1PF6.2	6743.1
3PF6.2	674310.
-2PF6.2	6.7431

If a FORMAT statement contains a P- specification, FORTRAN applies that scale factor to all succeeding F, E, and D- fields in that statement. In order to nullify this condition, the first F, E, or D- field following the P- specified field must contain an 0P specification. For example, the statement

```
FORMAT (I2, F6.2, 2PF7.3, E16.6, I6, D20.7)
```

will be processed as if it were written

```
FORMAT (I2, F6.2, 2PF7.3, 2PE16.6, I6, 2PD20.7)
```

Hence, what is needed is

```
FORMAT (I2, F6.2, 2PF7.3, 0PE16.6, I6, D20.7)
```

Skipped Fields

As pointed out in the first chapter, the programmer must make sure that his output is easily identified and read. Specifically, it is important that the numerical output quantities be separated by blanks so that there is no chance of overlap. We have seen that one way of providing such spaces is to provide for extra digits in field specifications. FORTRAN provides an additional means for spacing. This format specification takes the form

nX

where n is the number of spaces to be skipped. For example, the statements

```
      WRITE (6, 22) I, J, K
22    FORMAT (I6, I4, I6)
```

will produce as output

```
IIIIIIJJJJKKKKKK
  I   J    K
```

Changing the format specification to

```
22    FORMAT (I6, 5x, I4, 5x, I6)
```

will produce

```
IIIIIIbbbbbJJJJbbbbbKKKKKK
```

In addition to providing spaces between printed values, the X-specification can be used to center a line of output. Referring to the example above, let's say we want to center the 26 output characters (6 digits, 5 blanks, 4 digits, 5 blanks, 6 digits) on a 132-character print line. To achieve this we must move the output (132-26)/2 or 53 spaces to the right. Although the WRITE statement doesn't change, we'll include it here for continuity, along with the new FORMAT statement.

```
        WRITE (6, 22) I, J, K
22      FORMAT (53X, I6, 5X, I4, 5X, I6)
```

The X-specification can of course, be used with input as well as output statements. When reading data from punched cards, for example, an nX specification will cause the next n columns of the card to be ignored.

Let's look as some examples of FORMAT statements using the field specifications discussed above. (We won't bother with O-Conversion).

Suppose the following information is stored in memory:

X = 72.69417

Y = 131064.1

Z = .00077

I = 191

J = -3

K = 79

W = 55.6

and we write the following output statements:

```
      WRITE (6, 17) X, Y, Z, I, J, K, W
17    FORMAT (1X, F10.5, F10.1, F8.5, I4, I2, I3, F6.1)
```

This will result in the following line being printed, starting in the second column on the print sheet (the first column is always reserved for a special purpose, which we'll cover later):

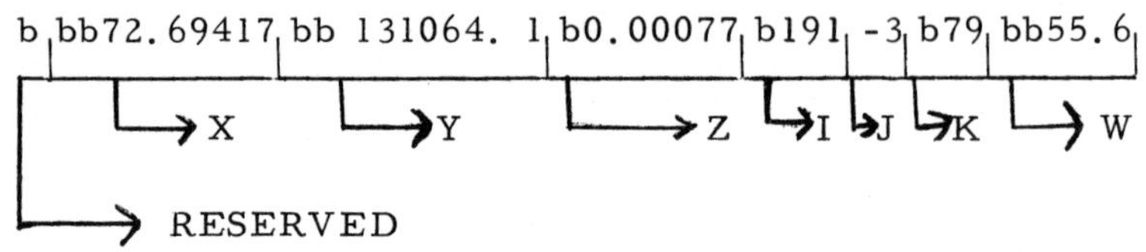

Using the same values, suppose we had written

```
      WRITE (6, 17) X, Y, Z, I, J, K, W
17    FORMAT (1X, F12.5, F12.1, E12.5, I6, I4, I5, F8.1)
```

This would produce a line looking like

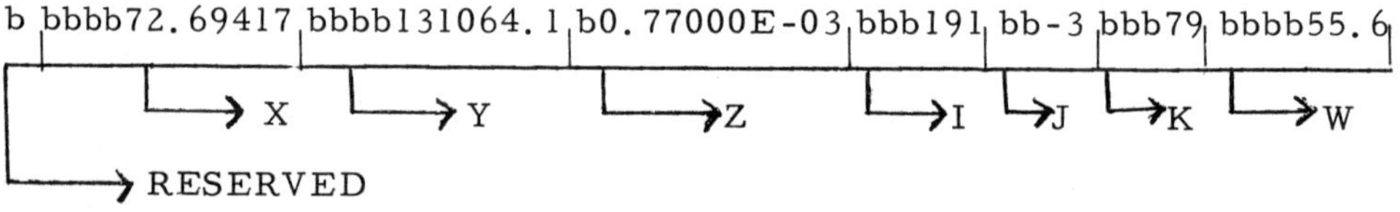

Thus, by increasing the field sizes or using skipped fields we can provide space between our output values, making them easier to read. This can be done up to a point: The printer can produce a line of up to 132 characters (or columns), the first of which is reserved, as was pointed out before. Thus a FORMAT statement cannot set up more than 131 columns of writing without a signal to go to the next line. This signal is a slash (/) and can appear only between field specifications, not in the middle of one. More about this a little later.

Let's set a new group of values:

X = 61.3974

Y = 80.3003

Z = 59.624

I = 17

J = 8

K = -26

W = .000004

If we write

```
        WRITE (6, 14) X, Y, Z, I, J, K, W
14      FORMAT (1X, 3F9.4, 3I3, E13.6)
```

we'll get

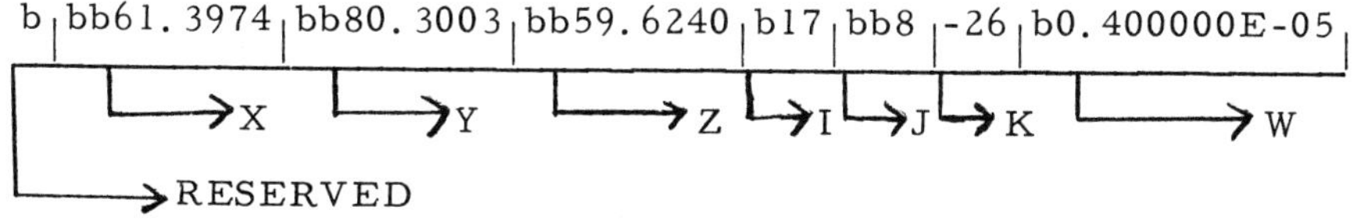

As a final example, let's throw together a line of output containing the following:

Y	(single precision)	-6.7
A	(double precision)	1467.44664467
I	(Integer)	16452
J	(Integer)	0
C	(complex)	14.64 - 32.0i
Z	(single precision)	0

```
      WRITE (6, 27) Y, A, I, J, C, Z
27    FORMAT (5X, F5.2, 2X, D15.8, 3X, 2I6, 2F6.2, 2X, F3.0)
```

The resulting output will be

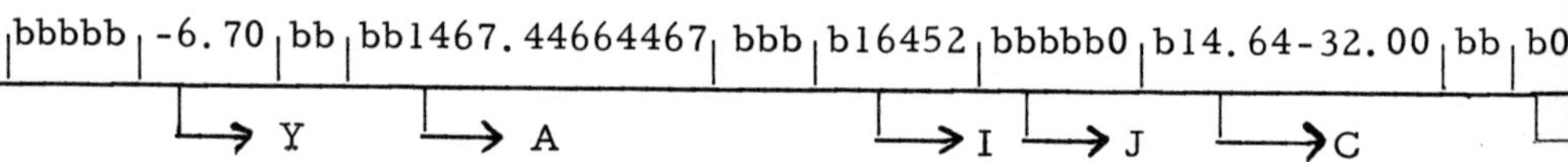

Short Forms for FORMAT Statements

We've seen previously that if we have several identical field specifications in succession, we can use a multiplier in front of the first one and simplify the statement. Thus

FORMAT (I5, I5, I5, I5, I5, I5)

can be written

FORMAT (6 I5)

This is true for all types of specifications. If a sequence of several specifications is repeated, parentheses are used to shorten the forms:

```
FORMAT (I5, 7X, I5, 7X, I5, 7X)
```

can be shortened to

```
FORMAT (3 (I5, 7X))
```

Extending this, we can see that the statement

```
FORMAT (F7.2, 2(3X, F11.3, 2X, I3), E11.4)
```

will produce values in the following order:

F7.2, 3X, F11.3, 2X, I3, 3X, F11.3, 2X, I3, E11.4.

The use of parentheses can also be applied to sets of format specifications for infinite repetition. If no coefficient is included in front of the parentheses enclosing the specifications, FORTRAN will continue repeating those specifications until the list given in the READ or WRITE statement is exhausted. As an example, suppose we want to read from a card a list of values consisting of a single precision floating point number of the form XXX.XX followed by a series of eight three-digit integers. This could be written as an ordinary FORMAT statement:

```
      READ (5, 27) X, (N(I), I = 1, 8)
27    FORMAT (F5.2, 8I3)
```

or in the alternate form

```
        READ (5, 37) X, (N (I), I = 1, 8)
    37  FORMAT (F5.2, (I3))
```

With this FORMAT statement, the program will read one floating point number following which it will read and store as many three-digit integers (eight in this case). This comes in handy for reading or writing variable amounts of information, as in the following example:

```
        READ (5, 41) M, X, (N (I), I = 1, M)
    41  FORMAT (I3, F5.2, (I3))
```

The two statements shown above are set up to read a card containing a three digit integer which is then used to determine how many values of N are to be read from that same card.

Multiple Record Formats

The types of FORMAT specifications covered to this point allow programs to accept a wide variety of input data, producing a similarly wide range of output. These specifications, however, provide for transmission of single records without variation in format.

Such variation is possible by using multiple record specifications. The start of a new record (new card or line of print) is indicated by the slash (/) appearing in a FORMAT statement between field specifications. When associated with input, the slash is a signal to read a new card. When used with output, the slash causes the start of a new line. To illustrate:

```
      WRITE (6, 12) X, Y, I, Z, W
12    FORMAT (15X, F7.2, 20X, E14.7, 15X, I7/25X, F9.4, 16X, F6.3)
```

This output combination will result in a two-line print, with the first line containing X, Y and I and the second line containing Z and W. Every time this WRITE statement is executed, these two lines will be written.

Suppose we want to read single values of X, Y and N, followed by arrays of Z and W. The following instructions would set this up:

```
      READ (5, 12) X, Y, N, (Z(I), W(I), I = 1, N)
12    FORMAT (20X, F7.2, 15X, F6.2, 15X, I6/(F6.2, 5X, F8.4))
```

The parentheses around the field specifications following the slash are indications to FORTRAN that X, Y, and N are to be read once from the first card. All subsequent cards will be interpreted as having values of Z (I) and W (I). Thus, these instructions will cause N + 1 cards to be read:

First Card contains X, Y, and N

Second Card contains Z_1 and W_1

Third Card contains Z_2 and W_2

etc.

$(N + 1)^{th}$ Card contains Z_n and W_n

The slash can also be used to indicate blank output, i.e., to skip lines. Going back to the previous example, suppose we wanted to print the values of X, Y and N on one line, skip a line, and then print lines containing Z (I) and W (I). We could set this up as follows:

```
    WRITE (6, 11) X, Y, N (Z(I), W(I), I = 1, N)
11  FORMAT (36X, F7.2, 15X, F6.3, 15X, I6//(59X, F6.2, 5X,F8.4))
```

Thus we can state in general terms that if we have N slashes in succession between format specifications, we will get N-1 blank lines, or, in the case of input, N-1 cards skipped before the next one is read.

Special Techniques for Punched Output

In the section dealing with floating point specifications, it was indicated that an E, F, or D-output format would produce a value with an appropriately located decimal point. This is true regardless of the output medium being used. Consequently, a statement calling for the transmission of real output to a punch will produce punched cards with decimal points. If it is wished to avoid this, i.e., to produce punched floating point data with an implied decimal point, an effective method can be applied by taking advantage of FORTRAN's real-integer conversion routines. An example will illustrate this:

Suppose we have a single precision variable called X whose current value is 118.514. Ordinarily, an F8.3 specification could be used to print or punch this value. In this case, however, we wish to eliminate the decimal point. First, we multiply X by the appropriate power of 10 to eliminate the decimals and convert to integer form. Then, we can punch the value as an integer (let's assign unit no. 7 to the punch). If we call the new integer variable J, we can write

```
      X = X * 10** 3
      J = X
      WRITE (7, 12) J
12    FORMAT (I6)
```

Thus, X is multiplied by 1000, giving a value of 118514. Since X is now an integer in floating point form, no significant digits are lost by truncation when conversion takes place. The I6 specification then produces the value in the first six columns of a punched card. Since the computation takes place prior to conversion, the first two steps in the example above can be combined:

```
J = X *10** 3 or J = 1000. *X
```

L-Conversion

The specification

Lw

is used to read in or write out logical information. When associated with input, Lw will cause FORTRAN to scan the next w characters coming in. The first T or F encountered will result in .TRUE. or .FALSE. being stored in the appropriate logical variable listed in the READ statement. When used with an output statement, Lw will cause FORTRAN to insert a T or F on the output line preceded by w-1 blanks for each logical variable as specified in the list of the WRITE statement. Thus, for example, if we wish to write three logical variables T, U, and V, whose respective values are .TRUE., .FALSE. and .FALSE., the statements

```
      WRITE (6, 11) T, U, V
11    FORMAT (6X, 3L6)
```

will produce

```
bbbbbb bbbbbT  bbbbbF  bbbbbF
       ______  ______  ______
         T       U       V
```

H-Conversion

FORTRAN provides means for transmitting non-numeric information to and from the central processor. Capability is included for handling characters singly or in groups, as well as literal data.

One of these is the H-conversion, which takes the general form

wH

When FORTRAN encounters this specification with a WRITE statement, the w characters (including blanks) immediately following the "H" are transmitted as dictated by the specification's place in the FORMAT statement. Suppose we wanted to print the following heading, centered, on a line:

CAPSULE EVALUATION PROGRAM

This heading is 26 characters long, including the space between words. To center this in our 132-column field we'll leave 53 blank columns to the left of the heading. The output statements, then, would look like this:

```
        WRITE (6, 29)
29      FORMAT (53X, 26CAPSULEbEVALUATIONbPROGRAM)
```

(the b's as usual, indicate blanks).

Notice that no list was given with the WRITE statement. When the H-conversion is used, FORTRAN prints what is actually in that part of the FORMAT statement, thus eliminating the need for a list.

Now let's take this a step further. Suppose we want to print a sentence containing a variable value:

FINAL FLUID VOLUME IS XXX. XXX CU. CM.

where XXX. XX is a quantity to be filled in by computation. As such, it is a real variable stored in a place called VOL. Let's center the heading first. Counting blanks between words, leaving blanks on either side of the value and allowing 8 columns for the value (6 digits, decimal point and sign), we get a heading length of 38 columns. To center, we'll leave 47 blank spaces to the left of the heading. The part of the heading preceding the value requires 22 columns, and the part after the value requires 8 columns. Our output statements will look like this:

```
        WRITE (6, 14) VOL
14      FORMAT (47X, 22HFINALbFLUIDbVOLUMEbISb, F8. 3, 8HbCU.bCM.)
```

A wrong count in front of the H in a field specification will prevent compilation, so count carefully and remember to include blanks, decimal points, signs, etc., as part of the count.

When the H-conversion is used with a READ statement, FORTRAN takes w characters of input and uses them to replace the w literal characters in storage. The statements

```
        READ (5, 24)
24      FORMAT (5X, 6HbAWAYb)
```

will cause FORTRAN to take the six characters from columns 6-11 of a punched card and place them in that location of storage which previously contained the six characters "bAWAYb".

Spacing on the Printer (Carriage Control)

It was pointed out previously that the first column of the printed page never contains any actual printing when FORTRAN is being used. It is reserved, instead, for controlling the print carriage. Several codes are available for different purposes. These are as follows:

Signal	Function
blank or /	Single space before printing.
0	Double space before printing.
-	Triple space before printing.
1	Start a new page.
+	No space before printing.

(There are additional symbols which are for special control and need not concern us now.)

Let's go back to our heading which says

CAPSULE EVALUATION PROGRAM

This might be the first thing printed in some program and as such we want it at the top of a new page. Our output statements would say

```
      WRITE (6, 29)
29    FORMAT (1H1, 53X, 26HCAPSULEbEVALUATIONbPROGRAM)
```

FORTRAN, encountering the (1H1) would not print a "1" in the first column. Instead, it would "restore the carriage" to the top of a new page.

A-Conversion

This type of conversion, stated in the form

Aw

will read w characters of alphameric data into storage under a variable name, or write it out from storage. The maximum number of characters handled by an A-specification (w) depends on the internal structure of the particular processor. A summary of these limits for various systems is given in Table XVII.

As an example, suppose we were working with a version of FORTRAN IV in which w_{max} = 8 and we had the following situation: We have two arrays in storage, each consisting of 411 elements. The first array, called PRTLST, is a list of part numbers, each number having the form RNNN-R where R is some letter and N is some digit (a typical part number might be B736-N). The second array, called NMANY,

Table XVII

Limitations on Number of Characters Accepted in a Single A-Specification

A. Input

Computer Type	w_{max}	If $w < w_{max}$	If $w > w_{max}$
IBM 360, RCA SPECTRA 70	8 or 16*	w characters are read and stored left-justified, followed by $(w_{max}-w)$ blanks blanks.	the first $(w-w_{max})$ characters are skipped and the w_{max} rightmost characters read.
CDC 3600/3400	8		
CDC 3200 UNIVAC III	4 or 8*		
RCA 3301	10		
IBM 7040/7044/7090/7094, PHILCO 2000	6		
IBM 1401,1410,1440,1460	Variable		

B. Output

Computer Type	w_{max}	If $w < w_{max}$	If $w > w_{max}$
IBM 360 RCA SPECTRA 70	8 or 16*	w characters preceded by $(w_{max}-w)$ blanks are transmitted to the designated output device.	the first w_{max} characters are transmitted and the remainder are lost.
CDC 3600/3400	8		
CDC 3200, UNIVAC III	4 or 8*		
RCA 3301	10		
IBM 7040/7044/7090/7094, PHILCO 200	6		
IBM 1401,1410,1440,1460	Variable		

*Depending on whether the variable name is integer or real.

contains the current inventory. Thus the contents of NMANY (37) gives the number of parts having the part number stored in PRTLST (37), etc. A program to read in a part number, find the proper inventory and print the part number plus the inventory, would look as follows (assume the part number (call it PRTEST) is punched in cols. 1-6 on a card):

```
        READ (5, 8) PRTEST
  8     FORMAT (A6)
        DO 30 I = 1, 411
        IF (PRTEST.EQ.PRTLST (I) GO TO 40
 30     CONTINUE
        WRITE (6, 10) PRTEST
 10     FORMAT (10X, 24HYOUbASKEDbFORbPARTbNO.bb,
                    A6, 25Hbb.bHEbAIN'TbONbOURbLIST.)
        GO TO 60
 40     WRITE (6, 20) NMANY(I) PRTEST
 20     FORMAT (10X, 11HTHEREbAREbb, I8, 21HbbUNITS
                    bOFbPARTbNO.bb, A6)
 60     STOP
        END
```

After having read the part number this program compares the part number with each of those in its stored list until it finds the proper one, at which point the desired output is printed. If an unacceptable part number is submitted an error message is provided. Thus, it the program found 134 pieces of part no. C414-W, the output would read

```
THEREbAREbb |bbbbb134| bbUNITSbOFbPARTbNO.bb |bbC414-W|
             NMANY(I)                           PRTLST(I)
```

R-Conversion

CDC 3600/3400/3200 FORTRAN IV provides an additional alphameric specification in the form of the R-conversion. Use of this specification gives the programmer additional control over the internal storage of non-numeric data. The specification, whose general form is

FORMAT (Rw)

operates just like A-conversion with these exceptions: When used with an input statement, and w is less than w_{max}, w characters, preceded by $(w_{max}-w)$ zeros. When used with an output statement and w is less than w_{max}, the w characters are written out preceded by $(w_{max}-w)$ zeros. Suppose the characters HOOBOY and HOOHA are punched in columns 1-6 and 1-5 of two consecutive cards and were using a machine for which $w_{max} = 8$. As a result of the statements

```
      READ (5, 9) STORE1
9     FORMAT (A6)
      READ (5, 10) STORE2
10    FORMAT (R5)
```

STORE1 will contain HOOBOYbb and STORE2 will contain 000HOOHA.

T-Specification

The IBM 360 FORTRAN IV compiler includes a T-specification which offers increased flexibility in transmitting input or output. The general form is

```
FORMAT (Tw)
```

where w in this case is the number of characters preceding the first character in a data field to be transmitted. With input, for example, the statements

```
        READ (5, 12) X, Y
12      FORMAT (T6, F7.2, T30, 'WOW', T20, F6.3)
```

would cause the machine to read a card, skip the first five columns, and, starting with column 6, store the next seven digits in X, in the form XXXXX.XX. Then, starting in column 30, it would read the next three characters (cols. 30, 31, 32) and store them in the locations previously containing the characters WOW. Then starting in col. 20, it would read the next six digits (cols. 20-25) and store them in Y as YYY.YYY. Note that the order is not important.

With output, the w in the T-specification tells FORTRAN where to place the information in the output field. Suppose we were printing X and Y from the above example . Our statements

```
        WRITE (6, 14) X, Y
14      FORMAT (T6, F9.2, T30, 'WOW', T20, F8.3)
```

would produce

```
bbbbb|bXXXXX.X|bbbbb|bYYY.YYY|bbWOW
     |___X____|     |___Y____|
```

Literal Data in FORMAT Statements

FORTRAN IV compilers for computing systems such as the IBM 360, RCA SPECTRA 70, GE 625/635 and CDC 3600/3400 permit the inclusion of literal data as part of format specification statements. Actual literal constants can be specified without the necessity of counting the number of characters to be transmitted. The general form for the literal specification is

FORMAT ('LOOKbHERE')

where 'LOOKbHERE' is a literal constant within the legal length limits. When used with a READ statement, FORTRAN counts the number of characters between the apostrophes, reads that many characters from the designated input unit, and places the characters in those storage locations wherein it finds information identical to that within the apostrophes. Thus, in the example above, (FORMAT('LOOKbHERE')) FORTRAN IV reads nine characters (blanks count) and places them in those storage locations which previously contained the nine characters LOOKbHERE. (Note: CDC 3600/3400 FORTRAN IV looks for asterisks (*) rather than apostrophes for bracketing literal formats).

When used with a WRITE statement, this type of format causes FORTRAN IV to transmit the characters within the apostrophes (or asterisks) to the designated output unit. Suppose we had the combination

```
      READ (5, 11)
11    FORMAT ('bbbbbbbb')
      WRITE (6, 11)
```

and a card with the characters IbGOTbIT punched in columns 1-8. The three statements shown above would cause the first eight columns to be read and stored replacing the eight blanks previously designated. The subsequent WRITE statement would send FORTRAN IV to those same locations from which it would get and print what is currently there, namely, IbGOTbIT.

Variable Formats

In many instances it is desirable to write programs which are sufficiently general so that they may be used for a variety of applications. A statistical analysis, for example, could serve equally well for medical, metallurgical, aerospace or chemical problems. Since data may come in from various sources, the programmer may not be able to set his input format according to any one, prearranged scheme. The variables may change in length and/or column location from problem to problem.

FORTRAN IV provides the capability for handling variable formats by allowing the entrance of a FORMAT statement as part of the input. This is done by permitting the use of a variable name instead of a statement number in a READ statement. Thus, we need not always write

READ (5, 17) list or READ (5, 22) list.

Instead we can write

READ (5, DATFMT) list or READ (5, FMT) list

or some name other than DATFMT or FMT which we might choose. This name then refers to a place in memory where an actual FORMAT statement is stored after being read in previously. Since FORTRAN IV will automatically look for a FORMAT statement in the designated area in storage, it is not necessary to include the word FORMAT on the statement being read in. That is, we can start with our left parenthesis right in column 1 and continue. As an example, let's consider a machine whose memory is constructed to accommodate up to six characters in a word. Furthermore, let's assume that an array consisting of 12 words of memory has been reserved under the name VARMT. With these ground rules in mind, let's write a typical program segment for reading in and using a variable format:

	Statement	Comment
	READ (5, 11) VARFMT	The alphameric character punched in columns 1-72 of a card are read in and stored as 12 groups of six characters each in VARFMT (1) thru VARFMT (12).
11	FORMAT (12A6)	
	READ (S, VARFMT) X, Y	Another card is read using the format information stored in VARFMT and the two pieces of information thus transmitted are stored in X and Y.

Now let's get more specific. Suppose we used the input statement above to read the following two cards:

```
Col. 1
     ↓
     (3X, F7.3, 4X, F5.1)
     60974435128149321792604
```

Our situation in memory would look as follows:

Variable Name	Contents
VARFMT (1)	(3X, F7
VARFMT (2)	.3, 4X,
VARFMT (3)	F5.1)b
VARFMT (4)-VARFMT (12)	All blanks
X	7443.512
Y	3217.9

Note: The READ statement does not in itself reserve the necessary storage for VARFMT. Reservation of storage areas must be made using the DIMENSION statement which is covered in the next chapter. Variable formats can, of course, be used for output purposes also.

The Generalized READ Statement

IBM 360 FORTRAN includes a generalized READ statement which allows the programmer to specify, at his option, additional information about program decisions regarding the input. The general form for the full statement is

```
READ (N, M, END=J, ERR=K) list
```

where N, M, and "list" have the meanings previously described (Chapter V). J is the statement number to which the program is to go after reading the last piece of data and K is the statement number to which a transfer is to be made if an error condition is encountered during the reading operation (END= J and/or ERR= K) may, of course, be omitted. Note that it is up to the programmer to provide the means for recognizing the last piece of data and for defining and recognizing an error in the data.

Problems

1. Read values of V, W, X, Y, and Z from a card.

2. Read and store a list of 376 X's.

3. Write the 17th column of a 20 x 25 matrix of Y's.

4. Write the even-numbered rows of a 21 x 15 matrix of J's.

5. Write a program which prints the contents of columns 2-80 of any card having an L in column 1. Center the print on the line and skip a line between printing.

6. Write a program which reads N numbers into storage, arrange them in descending order and print them 6 to a line. The number may range in value from .0001 to 99999.

7. Write a program to generate and print prime numbers (one to a line) up to some limit L.

8. A doctor doing a growth study has punched cards containing the following information:

Column No.	Item	Form
1 - 3	weight in lbs.	XXX.
4 - 5	height in inches	XX.
9	sex	M or F

No decimal points are punched.

Write a full program, including input/output, to compute and print the following output page:

GROWTH STUDY

Place for Doctor's Name

Place for Date

AVERAGE WT. FOR	XXX BOYS IS	XXX. X LBS.
AVERAGE WT. FOR	XXX GIRLS IS	XXX. X LBS.
AVERAGE WT. FOR	XXXX CHILDREN IS	XXX. X LBS.
AVERAGE HT. FOR	XXX BOYS IS	XX. X IN.
AVERAGE HT. FOR	XXX GIRLS IS	XX. X IN.
AVERAGE HT. FOR	XXX CHILDREN IS	XX. X IN.
AVERAGE HT. /WT. FOR	XXX BOYS IS	X. XXX IN. /LB.
AVERAGE HT. /WT. FOR	XXX GIRLS IS	X. XXX IN. /LB.
AVERAGE HT. /WT. FOR	XXXX CHILDREN IS	X. XXX IN. /LB.

MAXIMUM BOYS	HT. /WT. IS	X. XXX IN. /LB.
MAXIMUM GIRLS	HT. /WT. IS	X. XXX IN. /LB.
MIMIMUM BOYS	HT. /WT. IS	X. XXX IN. /LB.
MINIMUM GIRLS	HT. /WT. IS	X. XXX IN. /LB.

Chapter VI

Specification Statements

In setting up many of the programs and program segments in previous chapters we have assumed that areas in memory were somehow made available for storing certain variables and lists of variables. This chapter will deal with the methods used in FORTRAN programming for allocating storage and defining the nature of things to be stored.

The DIMENSION Statement

In order to handle arrays properly, FORTRAN must reserve space for them when it is compiling. This is done with the DIMENSION statement using the general form

```
DIMENSION A (L, M, N, etc.)
```

where A is the name of the array and L, M, and N are the dimensions of the largest array that is expected to be used in the program. If M and N are omitted, the array is merely a one-dimensional list. Any number of arrays may be set up in the same DIMENSION statement. Thus

```
DIMENSION A(4, 7), B(5), C(100)
```

is perfectly fine. The numbers in the parentheses must be unsigned integer constants. Since this statement allocates storage, it must precede any executable statements in which the dimensioned variable is used. To play it safe, it is usually best to put all DIMENSION statements at the beginning of a program. One precaution should be mentioned here: It is not a good idea to reserve single words in storage with DIMENSION statements such as

```
DIMENSION Y(1), Z(1), J(1)
```

This is inefficient in terms of how such statement are compiled. A more suitable way would be to use initializing statements like

```
Y = 0.
Z = 0.
J = 0
```

If the variable being dimensioned is of the type which requires more than one storage location for a single value (such as complex or double precision) FORTRAN IV will determine the correct number of locations automatically. The programmer need only specify the number of elements. For example, if a program used an array of double precision elements called D which is to have 21 rows and 6 columns, the appropriate DIMENSION statement would be

```
DIMENSION D (21, 6)
```

FORTRAN will multiply the two length values, thus determining that D will have no more than 126 elements. Since each of these 126 elements is to be stored in double precision form, FORTRAN will automatically reserve 252 locations. How FORTRAN knows that D is a double precision array in the first place is something we are about to divulge.

Type Declaration Statements

These statements allow the programmer to specify by name those variables which are to be stored in a given form. By means of these type declaration statements, the programmer can identify complex, double precision, and logical variables. Furthermore, it is possible to override FORTRAN's built-in rule about certain letters being reserved for real variables, etc.

Explicit Type Statements

The general form for this statement is

$$\text{type B } (n_1, n_2, \text{ etc.})$$

where "type" is either INTEGER, REAL, DOUBLE PRECISION, COMPLEX, or LOGICAL,

B is the name of a specific variable or array

n_1, n_2, etc. are the dimensions for an array whose type is being specified.

Thus, if one wishes to set up an array of complex numbers, for example, a single statement can take care of reserving the necessary storage and letting FORTRAN know that the array is to be complex. If we want to reserve space for a 266-element array of complex numbers under the name CMPVAR, one statement such as

```
COMPLEX CMPVAR (266)
```

will do it. More than one variable may be specified in a single declaration, as in the statement

```
LOGICAL X, A, Z, HOWIS, WHAT1, WHICH(20, 20)
```

As a result of this declaration, X, A, Z, HOWIS, WHAT1, and a 20 x 20 array called WHICH will be treated as logical variables throughout the entire program.

The type declaration statements may also be used to override FORTRAN's rule concerning variables beginning with certain letters. With such statements as

REAL I, J, MASS, NUMBER
INTEGER COUNT(10), TOTAL, B, E

the variables in the lists will be treated in the specified mode for the entire program. Or, putting it another way, if a given variable is not listed in a type declaration statement, it will be considered an integer if its name begins with I, J, K, L, M or N. (Note that the UNIVAC III, IBM 1401, 1410, 1440, 1460, and the RCA 3301 do not allow for COMPLEX or DOUBLE PRECISION specifications. In addition, the IBM 1401 FORTRAN does not include the LOGICAL type declaration.)

Expanded Explicit Type Statements

The IBM 360 version of FORTRAN IV provides capability for wider specifications to be given as part of type declaration statements. In addition to the listing of variable names to be treated as integers, logical, etc., the programmer can exercise some control over the allocation of storage, reserve sections of memory for arrays, and set initial values. We'll take a look at each feature by itself and then build up a full-blown explicit specification.

Ordinarily, without specific instruction, 360 FORTRAN assigns a preset number of memory locations to each type of variable as follows:

INTEGER - 4 locations
REAL - 4 locations
COMPLEX - 8 locations
LOGICAL - 4 locations

These may be changed by a statement of the form

Type * N list

where "Type: is either INTEGER, REAL, COMPLEX, or LOGICAL, N is the number of storage locations to be assigned, and "list" gives the names of the variables to be thus assigned. Table XVIII gives the values of N available for use in these declarations. The DOUBLE PRECISION declaration is also available but has no optional N (N always = 8).

Table XVIII

Allowable Length Changes for Variables in 360 FORTRAN

Type	N
INTEGER	2
REAL	8
COMPLEX	16
LOGICAL	1

Note that although multiple locations are assigned, once a group of locations are designated by a variable name, that group is treated as a single entity. Let's look at an example:

```
REAL * 8 X, INTER, SPEED, MSSFLW
```

This causes the compiler to assign eight storage locations to each of four real variables named X, INTER, SPEED, and MSSFLW, thus making each of them in effect a double precision variable. Had we written

```
REAL*8 X, INTER * 4, SPEED, MSSFLW
```

the compiler would assign eight locations to each variable in the list except for INTER, for which the usual four locations are specifically requested. On the other hand, if we know in advance that a certain integer variable will remain within a restricted range (up to 32767) we can restrict the amount of storage reserved for it. Thus,

```
INTEGER*2 COUNT1, COUNT2, COUNT3*4
```

will assign two locations to each of the variables COUNT1 and COUNT2 while allocating the standard four locations for integer variable COUNT3.

The extended explicit type declaration statement also can be used to include the function ordinarily performed by a DIMENSION statement. To do this, the programmer merely includes the dimensions of the array in the declaration statement as follows:

```
INTEGER COUNT (6, 6, 6)
```

This statement reserves 864 locations (6x6x6x4) for a three-dimensional integer array called COUNT. Had we written

```
INTEGER *2 COUNT (6, 6, 6)
```

only 432 locations would have been reserved.

One more capability is built into this type of statement in that it may be used to specify initial values for any or all of the variables in a declared list. For example, the statement

```
COMPLEX *16 ELEC/(17.4, 3.3)/
```

reserves 16 locations for a complex variable named ELEC and places an initial value of 17.4 + 3.3i in there. We can take this a step further. Suppose we wanted to specify a 5 x 5 integer array called HWMUCH and set the first 17 values to 0 and the remaining eight values to 19. Without these extended features, the necessary programming might look as follows:

```
         INTEGER HWMUCH
         DIMENSION HWMUCH (5, 5)
         DO 28 I = 1, 5
         DO 28 J = 1, 5
         IF((I.EQ.4AND.J.LT.3).OR.I.GT.4) GO TO 26
         HWMUCH (I, J) = 0
         GO TO 28
   26    HWMUCH (I, J) = 19
   28    CONTINUE
```

This can be done in one statement as follows:

```
         INTEGER HWMUCH (5, 5)/17* 0, 8* 19/
```

Just to make sure, let's look at a full-blown declaration statement:

```
REAL *8 LIFT/0.0/, GRAV * 4(12, 12), INDEX(14)/7* 2.0, 5*1.0, 2*0.0
```

The result of this statement will be that eight locations will be allocated under the name LIFT and a floating point zero will be stored there; 144 groups of four locations each (576 locations in all) will be assigned as a two dimensional real array called GRAV; 112 locations (14 x 8) will be assigned to a real array called INDEX in which the first seven groups of eight locations will initially contain floating point values of 2.0 the next five elements will be set to 1.0, and the remaining two will be initialized to zero.

Implicit Type Statements

The IBM 360 FORTRAN IV compiler also contains capability for more inclusive type declarations. Instead of specifying type for individual variables, the implicit statements allow the programmer to preassign the mode of all variables whose names begin with a given letter. The general form for this statement is

IMPLICIT Type * N (list)

where "Type" can be INTEGER, REAL, COMPLEX, or LOGICAL, * N indicates the length option as described under the extended explicit type statement, and "list" is a series of single alphabetic or special characters separated by commas, as in the statement

REAL * 8 (I, K, L, *)

As a result of this statement, all variables having names beginning with the letters I, K, and L or the symbol * will be assigned eight locations each and will be treated as real variables. An alternate form is

INTEGER (A-E)

This causes FORTRAN to treat all variables having names beginning with A, B, C, D or E as integers. Since the length option was not used, four locations would automatically be assigned to each variable.

One more thing. It is possible to combine several declarations in a single statement viz.,

```
INTEGER * 2 (A-C), LOGICAL(M-P, Z)
```

As a result of this statement, all variable names beginning with A, B, or C will be treated as integers and will each be assigned two locations. All variable names beginning with M, N, O, P or Z will be treated as logical variables.

The EQUIVALENCE Statement

FORTRAN gives the programmer a certain amount of control over the disposition of memory during the execution of his program. Some of this control is provided by the EQUIVALENCE statement, which allows the assignment of more than one name to a particular location in memory: Note that the programmer still doesn't know which absolute location he is assigning, but he can refer to it by more than one name and be sure that FORTRAN will use the same word of memory. The general form for this statement is

```
EQUIVALENCE (X, Y, I, J, etc.), (W, V, K, etc.)
```

where each of the arguments within the parentheses is a subscripted or non-subscripted variable (constants may <u>not</u> be used). This statement causes the variable names enclosed within a set of parentheses to be assigned to the same location. As indicated above, there can be any number of names included in one list, and any number of lists can be specified in a single statement (subject, of course, to the limitations on statement length). There is no restriction as to the type of variable which can be equivalenced. However, if variables of different length are equivalenced, the programmer must keep track of the storage allocation under each variable name. Some illustrations will help to clarify this. Suppose we wrote

```
LOGICAL X
REAL *8 J
EQUIVALENCE (SPEED, MIN, J, X)
```

Since the variables SPEED and MIN are not specified in type declaration statements, the built-in rules will make SPEED a single precision real variable and MIN a standard length integer variable. J, because of the type declaration, will be a single precision real variable like SPEED. X will be a logical variable, as indicated. Now, as a result of the equivalence statement, the same location in storage will be assigned to and can be referenced by any of the four names. The name used at a given point in the program will determine how FORTRAN will interpret the contents of that location. Had we written

```
LOGICAL X
REAL * 8 J
EQUIVALENCE (J, X, MIN, SPEED)
```

the names X, MIN, and SPEED would each be assigned to the first four (high order) locations of J. This type of statement comes in handy in large programs where the programmer is through with a variable and wants to use its location for some subsequent purpose. (Note that IBM 1401/1440/1460 FORTRAN IV does not allow the use of mixed modes in an EQUIVALENCE list.)

EQUIVALENCE statements may also be used with subscripted variables in two ways: Single variables can be equivalenced with single elements of arrays, or entire arrays or portions of arrays may be equivalenced with each other. Let's consider the first instance:

```
DIMENSION B (8)
EQUIVALENCE (A, B (5))
```

This sequence will result in the assignment of A and the fifth element in a one-dimensional array called B to the same location, so that we can imagine that portion of memory as follows:

B(1)	B(2)	B(3)	B(4)	B(5)	B(6)	B(7)	B(8)
				A			

This works the same way with multidimensional arrays except that we must keep in mind the method in which FORTRAN stores arrays (page 79). For example, the statements

```
DIMENSION C (2, 4, 3)
EQUIVALENCE (Y, X, C (2, 2, 1))
```

will assign the same location to Y, X, and the element in the first block, second column, second row of array C. In conventional notation, as shown previously in Chapter III, this array would be listed in the order

C(1, 1, 1), C(1, 1, 2), C(1, 1, 3), C(1, 2, 1), C(1, 2, 2), C(1. 2, 3),
C(1, 3, 1), C(1, 3, 2), C(1, 3, 3), C(1, 4, 1), C(1, 4, 2), C(1, 4, 3),
C(2, 1, 1), C(2, 1, 2), C(2, 1, 3), <u>C(2, 2, 1)</u>, C(2, 2, 2), C(2, 2, 3),
C(2, 3, 1), C(2, 3, 2), C(2, 2, 3), C(2, 4, 1), C(2, 4, 2), C(2, 4, 3),

so that C(2, 2, 1) is the 16th element in the array. FORTRAN stores the array in the order

C(1, 1, 1), C(2, 1, 1), C(1, 2, 1), <u>C(2, 2, 1)</u>, C(1, 3, 1), C(2, 3, 1),
C(1, 4, 1), C(2, 4, 1), C(1, 1, 2), C(2, 1, 2), C(1, 2, 2), C(2, 2, 2),
C(1, 3, 2), C(2, 3, 2), C(1, 4, 2), C(2, 4, 2), C(1, 1, 3), C(2, 1, 3),
C(1, 2, 2), C(2, 2, 3), C(1, 3, 3), C(2, 2, 2), C(1, 4, 3), C(2, 4, 3),

thus making C(2, 2, 1) the fourth element in the array with respect to the way it's stored. With this in mind, we can write

```
DIMENSION C(2, 4, 3)
EQUIVALENCE (Y, X, C(5)
```

which accomplishes the same thing as the two statements in the previous example. (Note that the IBM 1401, PHILCO 2000 and RCA 3301 FORTRAN does not allow more than single subscripts in EQUIVALENCE statements.)

The second and more general case is that in which arrays or portions of arrays are equivalenced to each other. All that is necessary is to equivalence single elements from each array and the others will fall into place. For example, the statements

```
DIMENSION A(6), B(7)
EQUIVALENCE (A(3), B(1))
```

will produce the following assignments in memory:

A(1)	A(2)	A(3)	A(4)	A(5)	A(6)			
		B(1)	B(2)	B(3)	B(4)	B(5)	B(6)	B(7)

It is often advantageous to assign two names to the same array where one of the arrays is one-dimensional while the other is multidimensional, as in the following:

```
DIMENSION X(10), Y(2, 5)
EQUIVALENCE (X, Y)
```

The assigned memory will look as follows:

X(1)	X(2)	X(3)	X(4)	X(5)	X(6)	X(7)	X(8)	X(9)	X(10)
Y(1, 1)	Y(2, 1)	Y(1, 2)	Y(2, 2)	Y(1, 3)	Y(2, 3)	Y(1, 4)	Y(2, 4)	Y(1, 5)	Y(2, 5)

The EQUIVALENCE statement could just as well have been written

```
EQUIVALENCE (X(1), Y(1, 1)) or
EQUIVALENCE (X(1), Y(1))
```

Incidentally, there is a simple relationship for determining which position a particular element in a stored array occupies relative to the first element. If an array A is I rows by J columns by K blocks, and (i, j, k) is the subscript of a particular element in that array, the $(i, j, k)^{th}$ element is the $(i+(j-1)xI+(k-1)xIxJ)^{th}$ element in the stored array. Thus, if A is 5x4x6 and we want to see where A(3, 4, 4) is stored relative to A(1, 1, 1), it turns out to be the $(3+(4-1)x5+(4-1) \cdot x5x4)^{th}$ or the 78th element in A as stored in memory.

Let's set up one more example, this time one in which two two-dimensional arrays are equivalenced so that there is only partial overlap:

```
DIMENSION E(2, 2), G(2, 4)
EQUIVALENCE (E(1, 1), G(1, 4))
```

Our memory allocation schematic would be as follows:

G(1, 1)	G(2, 1)	G(1, 2)	G(2, 2)	G(1, 3)	G(2, 3)	G(1, 4)	G(2, 4)		
						E(1, 1)	E(2, 1)	E(1, 2)	E(2, 2)

Another way to represent this would be with the diagram below:

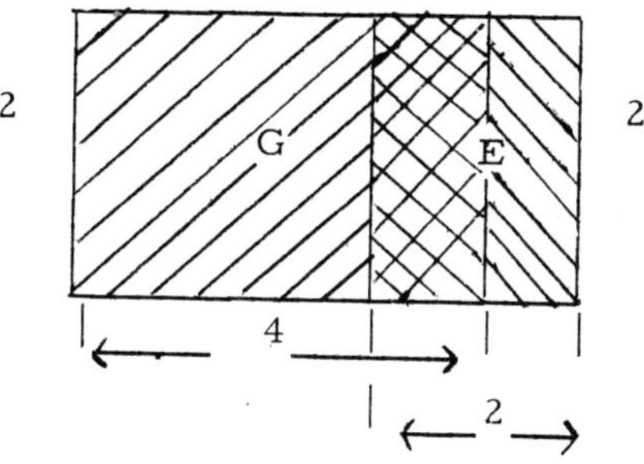

Since we haven't listed any rules for a while, let's enumerate a few with respect to EQUIVALENCE statements:

1. There must be consistency in all EQUIVALENCE statements in a given program. For example, we cannot say

```
DIMENSION A(5), B(5), C(5), D(5)
EQUIVALENCE (A(3), B(1), C(2)), (A(5), B(2), D(1))
```

Since A(3), B(1), and C(2) are equivalenced, the relative locations of these entire arrays have been defined as follows:

A(1)	A(2)	A(3)	A(4)	A(5)		
		B(1)	B(2)	B(3)	B(4)	B(5)
	C(1)	C(2)	C(3)	C(4)	C(5)	

We see that A(5) is assigned to the same location as B(3) (and also C(4) for that matter) so that the next list, which equivalences A(5) and B(2), is inconsistent and therefore invalid.

2. These statements may be placed anywhere in the program since they are non-executable. Care must be taken, however, to place them ahead of executable statements involving the variables in the equivalenced list. Otherwise it is easy to inadvertently destroy information stored in a given location before the program is finished with it.

3. If subscripts are used in equivalenced lists, they must be integer constants. Arguments must all be variables.

4. Two elements of the same array cannot be equivalenced.

The DATA Statement

In Chapter IV we covered the IF statement, which makes it possible to compare two numbers and let subsequent events be dictated by the outcome of such comparisons. Suppose, however, we wanted to compare two words or two letters and decide subsequent activity based on the equality of these words or letters. One way might be to read the word or letter in under a variable name and use that name for comparisons. For example, let us say that we wished to examine a set of cards in which a two letter code called CDLTRS is punched in columns 17 and 18. As a result of this examination we wish to print a count of all cards having WV in those columns. We could read the letters WV in as a special variable and test against it. Furthermore, let's say that there is no such code as XX, so that we can use this to test for the last data card:

```
      REAL LSTEST
      READ (5, 8) CDTEST,
 8    FORMAT (16X, A2)
      READ (5,  8) LSTEST
      N = 0
12    READ (5,  8) CDLTRS
      IF (CDLTRS.EQ.LSTEST) GO TO 26
      IF (CDLTRS.EQ.CDTEST) N = N + 1
      GO TO 12
26    WRITE (6,  27) N
27    FORMAT(1H1/51X, 25HTHE NUMBER OF WV CARDS = , I4)
      STOP
      END
```

Thus, we've read and stored the letters WV and XX. These were followed by a set of data cards, after which was included a card containing XX. Each incoming data card was tested twice--once for XX, in which case the program concluded that there were no more cards and proceeded to print the count. The second test was against the WV previously stored.

As illustrated by this example, it is necessary to read in non-numeric information as part of the data even though this information may be used as a constant for all program runs.

Many FORTRAN IV compilers (IBM 1401 FORTRAN does not provide this) relieve this problem by providing the DATA statement, whose general form is

$$\text{DATA X, Y, Z, etc /N} * \text{V.}, \text{M} * V_2, \text{etc /, A, B, C, etc /L} * V_3, N_4/$$

where X, Y, Z, A, B, and C are single variables, elements of arrays having constant subscripts, or array names; N, M and L are integer constants which indicate how many variables are to receive a certain initial value, and V_1, V_2, V_3, and V_4 are legal constants (real, integer, complex, double precision, logical, literal, or octal).

Going back to our WV example, we could write a DATA statement which said

```
DATA CDTEST/2HWV/, LSTEST/2HXX/
```

thus avoiding the two READ statements. For the IBM 360, the Hollerith specifications are replaced by literal constants, viz.

```
DATA CDTEST/'WV'/, LSTEST/'XX'/
```

Let's look at a sequence containing a more involved DATA statement:

```
LOGICAL B
DIMENSION A(10), B(4),
DATA X, Y, A/4*0.0, 8*1.1/, B/T, .FALSE., .TRUE., F/
```

Based on these statements, locations X, Y, and the first two elements in array A (A(1) and A(2)) will contain values of 0.0, A(3) through A(10) will each contain 1.1, and locations B(1), B(2), B(3) and B(4) will contain values of .TRUE., .FALSE., .TRUE., and .FALSE., respectively. (Two types of notation may be used for logical variables as shown.) When assigning alphameric characters in a DATA statement, care must be taken to provide sufficient storage for these characters. For example, in the IBM 360, where the four locations ordinarily assigned to a single variable accommodate eight characters, a statement like

```
DATA PLACE/'PUT IT HERE, CHARLIE'/
```

would not be accommodated without an additional statement in which adequate space were assigned, such as

```
DIMENSION PLACE(3)
```

On machines like the IBM 7040/44/90/94 in which each location holds six characters, the sequence would be

```
DIMENSION PLACE(4)
DATA PLACE/20HPUT IT THERE, CHARLIE/
```

We mentioned before that octal constants may also be specified in a DATA statement. The form is

```
DATA X/O nnnn/
```

where nnnn is the octal constant. The DATA statement in CDC 3600/3400/3200 FORTRAN uses a somewhat different form and can be linked with a COMMON statement. We'll cover this type of DATA statement together with the COMMON statement in the next chapter.

The NAMELIST Statement

FORTRAN compilers for the IBM 360, RCA SPECTRA 70 and GE 625/635 allow a type of shorthand for lists of variables which are referred to as a group in input/output statements. Furthermore, this feature provides for a simplified data input arrangement which under certain conditions may be advantageous. With the statement it is possible to specify a list of variables by a single collective name and then transmit that list (or any part of it) to or from the processor by using that name. The general form is

```
NAMELIST/SAM/A, B, C/MOE/X, Y, Z  etc.
```

when SAM is a name assigned to the list of variables A, B and C, and MOE is the name assigned to variables X, Y and Z. The variables included in a namelist may be single valued or entire arrays and any number may appear in a list. Names are assigned to these lists as they would be to variables (1-6 characters beginning with a letter) and are designated by enclosing them in slashes, as shown above. The NAMELIST must, of course, be defined before its use, and once it's been defined, the name can appear only in input/output statements. One more thing. A particularly gregarious variable may belong to more than one namelist. If two variable names are equivalenced and one is in a namelist, the other must appear there too.

Data associated with a namelist must be prepared in a certain way in order to be accepted by a namelist input statement. The easiest way to describe this will be to follow an example through its twistings and windings. Suppose we set up the following situation:

```
LOGICAL E(7)
DIMENSION B(10), I(6, 4)
NAMELIST/GROUP1/A, X, J, B, E, I
READ(5, GROUP1)
```

FORTRAN will then set up machine instructions to look for the name GROUP1 in the input, followed by values for any or all of the variables in GROUP1. Let's say we're reading from punched cards. The required format is as follows:

1. The first input card for a namelist must have Column 1 blank, and Column 2 must contain a + sign (& on some keypunches). The namelist name (GROUP1 in our example) is punched starting in Column 3.

2. This card is followed by an number of data cards, with information always starting in Column 2 (Column 1 is ignored).

The information is in the form

X(I, J) = K * V1,

where X is one of the variable names, I and J are constant subscripts which may or may not be included, V1 is a particular constant of appropriate type and K is an integer (optional) indicating to how many variables the value V1 is to be assigned. Note that a comma must be included after each assignment.

3. After the last data card comes a card with a + in Column 2 and the word END in Column 3-5. Sets for other namelists may then follow, as dictated by the program.

For our example, a typical data input package might look like this:

```
b+GROUP1
bX= 14.4, I= 22 * 6, 2*7, B(5)=9.61
bJ= 2, E= .TRUE., 2*F, 3.FALSE., T
b+END
```

As a result, X will contain 14.4, the first 22 values of I (I(1, 1) through I(4, 4)) will contain 6, the remaining I's (I(5, 4) and I(6, 4)) will be set to 7, B(5) will be 9.61 with the other B values undefined, J will be 2, and logical array E witll be TFFFFFT. Note that the complete namelist was not filled in. Also, since E was previously specified as an array but subscripts were not given in the input, FORTRAN will seek to fill the entire array with the values specified in the input.

When a namelist is used in an output statement, FORTRAN will produce a consecutive listing of the current values for each variable in the list. Array values will be produced in the order in which they are stored. If printed, the output will include a line with a plus sign and the namelist name, and one with +END. If punched, these standard first and last cards will be produced as part of the output. FORTRAN, in producing namelist output, will automatically format the data so that a sufficient number of digits are provided (such as using E-Conversion where necessary). Thus, in the case of our example, if we were to say

```
WRITE (6, GROUP1)
```

we would get

```
b+GROUP1
bA=0., X=14.4, J=2, B=0.,
    0.,        0., 0.,  9.61,
    0.,        0., 0.,  0.,
    0.,     E=T,   F,   F,
  I=6,          6,  6,    6,
    6,          6,  6,    6,
    6,          6,  6,    6,
    6,          6,  6,    6,
    6,          6,  6,    6,
    6,          6,  7,    7,
b+END
```

Problems

1. Set up a 20 x 40 array of double precision complex numbers called F.

2. Set up three arrays, called A, B and C, respectively, which will be stored as follows:

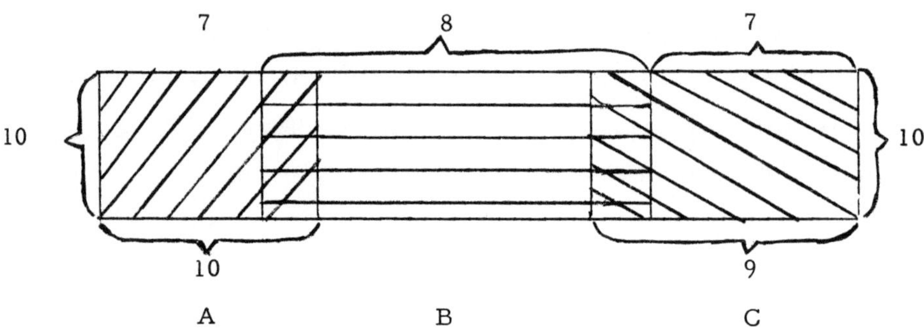

A is 10 x 10

B is 10 x 8

C is 10 x 9

The first three columns of B overlap the end of A

The first two columns of C overlap the end of B

3. Set up a 10 x 5 integer array called M and write the necessary statements to call the first column LOW, the second column MEDLOW, the third column MEDIUM, the fourth column MEDHI and the fifth column HIGH.

4. Use a single statement to set up a 10 x 20 integer array called HWMANY in which the first three columns contain zeroes and every odd-numbered column after that contains values of 7. All other columns (even-numbered columns above column 2) are to contain values of 4.

5. . The following data are available:

A is a real variable with a value of 11.4 .

B is a one-dimensional real array having six elements, the first two being zeroes and the rest 100.

I is a 2 x 3 array of integers with the first row having 4's and the second row containing 5's.

D is a six element logical array of cynical nature in which all the elements are false.

Construct a namelist called ALLALL containing these variables and show what the input cards would look like for a statement

READ(5, ALLALL)

6. A paper manufacturing company maintains a file of information on its products in the form of equivalent punched cards (that is, the information that would ordinarily be on a card is stored in the same form but on some magnetic device). The data thus stored consist of the following items:

Column No.	Item	Form
1 - 3	Paper Code Name	Three letters, e.g. YWT
4 - 7	Year Introduced	Four digit integer, e.g. 1927.
8 - 10	Thickness, thousandths of an inch	Three decimals, e.g. .006.
11 - 12	Grade of Paper	A number and letter, e.g. 3A.
13 - 14	Strength or Weight	A two digit integer, e.g. 80
15 - 17	Price per Square Foot	In dollars, to the thousandth of a dollar, e.g. .062.

Write a complete program which will provide any or all of the following types of information:

a) Given a thickness, grade, strength, or any combination of these, produce a list of available papers and their respective prices.

b) List the papers introduced during any number of specified years.

c) Find and identify the strongest paper for a given price, or the cheapest paper for a given strength.

d) Given one or more code names, list the characteristics of the appropriate papers.

e) Provide error messages for such contingencies as "no such code," "no paper this strong," "no paper this cheap" and any other appropriate situations.

All combinations of three letters could be codes except for XXY and YYX.

Chapter VII

Subprograms, Functions, and Subroutines

When we covered arithmetic statements we listed a number of function names which could be used directly in these statements to perform certain standard calculations. For example,

```
Y = SQRT (X)
```

will give the square root of X without the necessity for the programmer to specify the instructions for computing the square root. These instructions are already stored somewhere and FORTRAN references them as the need arises. A set of such instructions is called a subprogram. In addition to the standard functions provided by the FORTRAN library, mechanisms are available which allow the programmer to add those procedures or operations which find frequent use in his programs. By writing these procedures as subprograms, the programmer need only specify each set of instructions once, after which he can call any or all of those procedures any number of times in his main program. There are several types of subprograms, differing in terms of how much information they supply and how they are referenced.

Arithmetic and Logical Statement Functions

These are functions which can be defined by means of a single arithmetic or logical statement. For example, if we write the sequence

```
DNSTY (X) = X/(VOL*62.4)
Z = DNSTY (Y)
```

FORTRAN will calculate Z using Y/(VOL * 62.4). The variable named X used in the statement defining the function is called a dummy variable or dummy argument. As such it doesn't limit the function to one which will use only X. Now suppose we do not want to use VOL all the time. We could just as easily write a sequence like this:

```
DNSTY (X, VOL) = X/(VOL * 62.4)
Z = DNSTY (Y, W)
```

This will result in the calculation of Z as Y/(W*62.4). The dummy variables serve to tell FORTRAN how many variables are involved and in what mode they are to be. When a previously defined function is used in a statement, the variables listed in the parentheses must be in the same mode as those listed in the defining statement. It is also very important that the variables be listed in the order in which they are to appear in the expression. For example

```
CALC (X, Y, Z) = A *X* *2 + B *Y - 2.* Z
W = CALC (R, S, T)
```

will result in a W value of $AR^2 + BS - 2T$. If we had wanted $W = AT^2 + BR - 2S$, we would have written

```
W = CALC (T, R, S)
```

Since A, B and C were not among the list of dummy variables, the program will always use the current values of A, B and C whenever the CALC function is used. These variables,called parameters, must therefore be defined somewhere in the program prior to the function statement.

Statement function names are governed by the the same rules used for naming variables. None of the variables in the list of arguments nor in the expression to the right of the equal sign can be subscripted variables. (PHILCO 2000 and CDC 3600 FORTRAN allow constant subscripts.) Furthermore, no constants may appear in the list of arguments. However, the expression to the right of the equal sign may contain any legitimate terms, including references to previously defined statement functions. Thus, the following sequence is acceptable:

```
TRANS (X) = 3.* X**2 - SQRT (X)
SYNC (X, Z) = 14.4/X + 3.* TRANS (Z)
PHYS = 36.* Y - 0.4*SYNC (S, T)
```

PHYS will end up containing a quantity equal to

```
36.* Y - 0.4*(14.4/S + 3.*( 3.* T**2 - SQRT (T)))
```

Note that both the TRANS and SYNC functions were defined using X as one of the dummy arguments. The same variable name may be used as a dummy variable in any number of statement functions and then again as an actual variable in the main program without confusion.

Thus the statement function may be called merely by using the function name in some subsequent arithmetic or logical statement. These functions apply only to the particular program in which they are defined and do not become a part of the function library. If the function is widely used in a number of programs at a given computing center, it can be added to the permanent function library. The procedures for doing this, however, are beyond the scope of this book.

To round out the picture with regard to statement functions, let's look at one involving logical variables:

```
LOGICAL B, D
THNK (X, Y, Z) = X**2.NE.Y*Z
B = D.AND.THNK (S, T, U)
```

Encountering this, the program will compute S^2 and the product TU. If these two quantities are found to be unequal to each other, and a check of logical variable D shows it to be .TRUE., a value of .TRUE. will be placed in logical variable B.

All statement functions appearing in a program must be defined prior to the first executable statement in that program. If the function type is unspecified, FORTRAN will use the built-in rules for naming variables. Consequently, with most FORTRAN compilers, it is necessary to precede the function statements with type declaration statements for those cases where the type may be in doubt.

FUNCTION Subprograms

These subprograms provide output resulting from operations which cannot be completely described in a single statement. The group of statements which comprise one of these subprograms can be considered as a separate program. As such, they can be independently compiled. However the compilation must, of course, be included as part of the main program's object deck. The FUNCTION subprogram is called the same way as its simpler counterpart (the statement function), that is, by using it in an arithmetic or logical statement. As in the previous case, the subprogram is set up with dummy variables and terms (arguments) which serve to indicate the number and mode of variables to be used. They are replaced by the arguments in the statement using the function at execution time. The subprogram must begin with the statement

```
FUNCTION Name (list)
```

where "Name" is the title of the function and as such is the name which will call the subprogram in subsequent arithmetic or logical statements. Subprograms are named like variables (1 - 6 characters long beginning with a letter). If it is required to override the ordinary naming convention (I, J, K, L, M or N for first letters of subprograms which provide integer values) the type of function must be specified in the first statement. The types are defined as follows:

```
REAL FUNCTION Name (list)
COMPLEX FUNCTION Name (list)
INTEGER FUNCTION Name (list)
DOUBLE PRECISION FUNCTION Name (list)
LOGICAL FUNCTION Name (list)
```

This lets us write something like

```
REAL FUNCTION INTGRL (Y, X)
```

"List" in the general FUNCTION statement refers to a list of dummy arguments which FORTRAN will replace by an equal number of arguments of similar mode when the subprogram is called. These arguments may be constants, subscripted or non-subscripted variables, expressions, and/or names of other subprograms.

After the initial FUNCTION statement (with or without type specification as the need dictates) comes the group of statements needed to arrive at the function value. At least one of these statements must contain the function name as a single term on the left side of an = sign. All FUNCTION subprograms must end with a special statement which will allow FORTRAN to set up instruction to bring the function value back to the expression in which the function was used and to restore control to the main program. This is accomplished by writing

RETURN

at the end of the subprogram. Let's look at a simple subprogram:

It is desired to find DOSE (Z) when

for $Z < 3.4$ DOSE = $12Z^2 - 1.7$

for $Z \geqslant 3.4$ DOSE = $14Z^{2.2} - 1.95$

```
      REAL FUNCTION DOSE (Z)
      IF (Z.LT.3.4) GO TO 19
      DOSE = 1.4*Z**2.2 - 1.95
      RETURN
19    DOSE = 12.*Z**2 - 1.7
      RETURN
      END
```

Note that there are two returns. This program would be used in a statement such as the following:

```
STRGTH = A**2 + 2.*DOSE (X)
```

If an array is used as a dummy argument it must be the same maximum size and mode as the one used in a statement in the main program. That is, both the dummy and actual arrays must have been given the same size in a DIMENSION statement. Some versions of FORTRAN have exceptions to this as we'll see later.

SUBROUTINE Subprograms

This type of subprogram handles the contingencies which are not within the scope of the other subprograms. Thus far it was seen that it is possible to use more than one argument in a subprogram but only one value is returned each time the subprogram is called. Subroutines allow the return of more than one value or no values and may be considered as separate FORTRAN source programs which receive their input from another program and deliver their output to another program.

All subroutines must begin with the general statement

```
SUBROUTINE Name (list)
```

where "Name" is a designation (1-6 letters in length) for the subroutine, and "list" is a list of dummy arguments (not always needed) used in the subroutine. These, as in previous cases, are replaced with actual variables during execution. Subroutines must end with RETURN and END statements.

The calling of single output subprograms involves using the name in an arithmetic or logical statement. Subroutines, however, must be specifically called by the main program using the general statement

CALL Name (list)

where "Name" is the subroutine's name as defined in the first statement of the subroutine and "list" is an enumeration of the argument to be used. These must agree in mode, number and order with the dummy arguments set up in the subroutine. Actual arguments may include constants, subscripted or non-subscripted variables, arithmetic or logical expressions and names of other subprograms. Dummy arguments, however, are non-subscripted variables or array names. Subroutines (and other subprograms, for that matter) are usually written as distinct programs, complete with simple input-output statements. Once tested, the input-output is deleted and replaced with proper entry and return statements. The subroutine source instructions are then compiled together with those of the main program.

As an example, we shall set up a subroutine which takes the elements in a two-dimensional array A, squares them and puts them back in the same places:

Statement	Comment
SUBROUTINE SQARAY (A)	This names the subroutine and lists the dummy argument.
DIMENSION A (20, 20)	This dummy dimension statement defines the largest arrays to be handled. A similar statement for the actual argumen

Statement	Comment
	to be used must appear in the main program.
DO 20 I = 1, 20	These two DO loops perform the actual transformation and replacement.
DO 30 J = 1, 20	
30 A (I, J) = A (I, J)** 2	
RETURN	
END	

A CALL to SQARAY in the main program together with the name of the actual array to be transformed will perform the required transformation. Note that since a subroutine is compiled as if it were a separate program, statements in it need not have numbers which differ from those used in the main program.

It was pointed out earlier that subroutines need not return any values to the main program. Consequently, a CALL to a subroutine of such a type can be made without a list of arguments in the call statement. As an example, let's consider a subroutine which takes care of printing some standard headings at the top of a page:

```
      SUBROUTINE TOPPGE
      WRITE (6, 17)
17    FORMAT (1H1//)
      WRITE (6, 19)
19    FORMAT (10X, 8HPART NO., 10X, 12NO. INSTOCK,
                10X, 5HVALUE//)
      RETURN
      END
```

Now, in our main program, suppose we were printing information and counting the number of lines being printed (in a place called LINECT) so that when we got to 50 we would start a new page:

```
      IF (LINECT.LT.50) GO TO 24  (where 24 prints another line)
      LINECT = 0
      CALL TOPPGE
21    GO TO 24
```

If the result of the IF statement is such that the call to TOPPGE will be executed, then the program, upon reaching the RETURN statement in TOPPGE, will return control to the main program, at the statement immediately following the call, in this case, statement 21. From this we can infer that the RETURN statement has a fair amount of footwork behind it in that it automatically sets up a mechanism which specifies the point in the main program to which control is to be returned. It is this mechanism which allows the FORTRAN programmer to call a particular subroutine as many times as he wants from as many different points in his main program as he finds necessary.

The EXTERNAL Statement

In listing the types of actual arguments that can be used in a CALL to a subroutine, it was mentioned that such arguments may include arithmetic or logical expressions and names of other subprograms. If the latter is the case, FORTRAN must have a way of distinguishing subprogram names from variable names in a list of arguments. This is provided by the EXTERNAL statement, which says

```
EXTERNAL R, S, T, U, etc.
```

where R, S, T, and U represent names of subprograms which are to be used as arguments in other subprograms. A simple example will bring this into focus.

Suppose we wished to write a subroutine which had two specific uses: At one point in the main program, we wish to test a variable Y. If Y is between 0 and 1 we want the subroutine to return its square root in Y. Otherwise, Y is to be zero. At another point in the program, we want this same subroutine to test the quantity $3G^2 - 7$. If it turns out to be between 0 and 1, we would like the subroutine to return the inverse sine in G. If not, G should be zero. Our program would look as follows (assume Y and G are already in memory and have been defined):

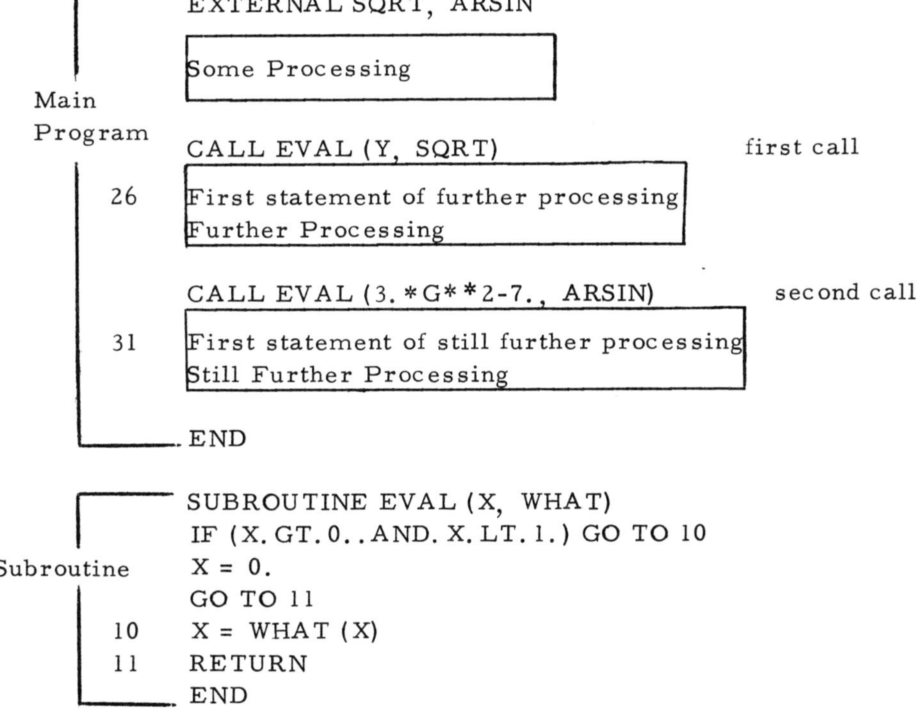

Let's look at the subroutine EVAL. Its first statement indicates that there are two dummy arguments. Since there is no DIMENSION statement, FORTRAN concludes that the arguments represent nonsubscripted (single-valued) variables. Further, from the way in which the argument WHAT is used it is decided that WHAT represents a dummy subprogram. When the first CALL is executed, the program replaces the dummy arguments with the actual real variable Y and the actual subprogram SQRT. SQRT is listed in an EXTERNAL statement, telling FORTRAN that this subprogram name will appear as an actual argument in a CALL. Then, as the subroutine is executed, WHAT (X) is calculated as SQRT (Y) (if the conditions are met). The RETURN statement sends control back to the main program at statement 26 with the appropriate value in Y. The second CALL replaces dummy argument X with the expression 3. *G**2-7., which is evaluated and used in the IF statement. If the expression is true, WHAT (X), which this time is ARSIN (3.* G**2-7.), is evaluated and placed in G. Otherwise, G is set at zero. In either case, control is returned to the main program at statement no. 31. Note that Z, which is not specified as a dummy argument, is treated as an actual parameter.

Expanded Capability in RETURN Statements

IBM 360 FORTRAN allows the use of statements in the form

```
RETURN n
```

where n is an integer constant or variable whose value specifies which of a series of statement numbers in the argument list is to be used. In this way, by giving several statement numbers in a CALL, the programmer can provide alternate return points after execution of a subroutine. This is not to be confused with the fact that a subroutine may have several points <u>from</u> which it can return. Here, we're talking about giving it several points <u>to</u> which it can return. A typical use might be as follows:

```
      SUBROUTINE MAYBE (X, Y, Z, * ,*)
      W = X**2 + 37 * Y/X * 2
      IF (W.LT.14.) GO TO 12
      IF (W.GT.14.) GO TO 22
      Z = W
      RETURN
12    Z = 1.2 *W
      RETURN 1
22    Z =0.86 * W
      RETURN 2
      END
```

Note that the dummy statement numbers are given as asterisks in the dummy argument list. As seen above, this subroutine provides three places from which to return based on the value of W. Furthermore, each of these returns may or may not be to a different place, depending on the call. If we write

```
CALL MAYBE (R, S, T, + 17, + 204)
```

the RETURN 1 statement will send control to statement 17, the RETURN 2 statement will send control to statement 204, and the RETURN will send control to the statement following the CALL statement. We could have written

CALL MAYBE (R, S, T, + 204, + 204)

thus narrowing the choice when appropriate. Note that the + (or &) in the CALL tells FORTRAN that the subsequent argument is a statement number.

The ENTRY Statement

When a call is made to a subroutine or a FUNCTION subprogram is used in an arithmetic or logical statement, control is turned over to the subprogram at the first executable statement immediately following the SUBROUTINE or FUNCTION statement. Aside from this normal operation, IBM 360, RCA SPECTRA 70 and CDC 3600/3400/3200 FORTRAN compilers allow these subprograms to be set up so that references to them from main programs may cause control to be turned over to them at more than one possible point. This is done by means of the ENTRY statement which takes the form

ENTRY PORTAL (list)

where PORTAL is the name assigned to the particular entry point into the subprogram and "list" is a string of dummy arguments required for the part of the subprogram from the entry point to the RETURN statement. This list need not be the same length as that specified in the initial SUBROUTINE or FUNCTION statement. Let's see how this might look:

```
      SUBROUTINE SEE (X, Y, Z)
      IF (X** 3. LT. Y *Z) GO TO 17
      WRITE (6, 22) X, Y, Z
22    FORMAT (10X, 3(F10.5, 10X))
      RETURN
17    ENTRY HERE (Y, Z)
      IF (Y. GT . 10 . * Z) GO TO 37
      WRITE (6, 32) Y, Z
32    FORMAT (10X, 15HX IS NEGLIGIBLE, 2 (10X, F10.5))
      RETURN
37    ENTRY BUSTER (Y)
      WRITE (6, 42) Y
42    FORMAT (10X, 22HX AND Z ARE NEGLIGIBLE, 10X, F10.5)
      RETURN
      END
```

Here we have a subroutine which prints partial or complete output based on the relative magnitudes of the variables. Because of the ENTRY statements, three types of calls may be made, resulting in transfer of control to the appropriate point:

```
CALL SEE (A, B, C)
CALL HERE (P, R)
CALL BUSTER (T)
```

Adjustable Dimensions in Subprograms

In the discussion dealing with allocation of memory for arrays (Chapter VI) it was pointed out that the array size specified in a DIMENSION statement must be a constant and should, therefore, be large enough to cover all contingencies, within the limitations of memory size. Furthermore, it was stipulated that when array names are used as dummy arguments in subprograms, a dummy DIMENSION statement must be included in the subprogram in which the specified array size matches that of the actual array to be used. Many FORTRAN IV compilers (IBM 7040/44/90/94, IBM 1410, and UNIVAC III not included) also allow the use of variable dimensions in subprograms. That is, the dimensions of a dummy array may be integer variables which are replaced by values coming in from the CALL statement as part of the list of actual arguments. As an example, let's look at a subroutine which interchanges the rows of a two-dimensional array so that the second row is switched to the first, the third to the second, and so on until the first row is moved to the last row:

```
        SUBROUTINE ROTATE (B, M, N, C)
        DIMENSION B (M, N), C (N)
        DO 24 I = 1, N
        C (I) = B (M, I)
        B (M, I) = B (1, I)
24      CONTINUE
        MM = M - 2
        DO 34 I = 1, MM
        DO 34 J = 1, N
        B (I, J) = B (I + 1, J)
```

```
34    CONTINUE
      DO 44 I = 1, N
      B (M - 1, I) = C (I)
44    CONTINUE
      RETURN
      END
```

In this particular subroutine, we used a separate one-dimensional array (C) for temporary storage of the last row of B, following which we moved the first row's contents into the last row. The double DO loop moved all the other rows down one row, except for the next-to-last one, which was brought in from C. A call to this routine might say

```
CALL ROTATE (X, 7, 7, Y)
```

or the dimensions could be integer variables which were previously defined:

```
CALL ROTATE (X, K, L, Y)
```

In either case, the main program must contain a specification statement of some kind which dimensions arrays X and Y so that they equal or exceed the arguments in the call.

One important precaution: Suppose we had a situation in our main program as follows:

```
DIMENSION X (4, 4), Y (4)
```

Other Statements

```
CALL ROTATE (X, 2, 3, Y)
```

From this call, we see that the programmer wants the subroutine to deal, at this point, with a shrunken version of array X. But, bearing in mind that FORTRAN stores the array by columns, observe that the shrinkage is most peculiar. Table XIX compares the full array as stored with the values referenced by the shrunken version used in this call to the subroutine:

Table XIX
Illustration of Adjustable Dimensions
Array X in Main Program is 4 x 4
Array X in Subroutine is 2 x 3

Main Program	Subroutine	Main Program	Subroutine
X (1, 1)	X (1, 1)	X (1, 3)	Not used
X (2, 1)	X (2, 1)	X (2, 3)	↓
X (3, 1)	X (1, 2)	X (3, 3)	
X (4, 1)	X (2, 2)	X (4, 3)	
X (1, 2)	X (1, 3)	X (1, 4)	
X (2, 2)	X (2, 3)	X (2, 4)	
X (3, 2)	Not used	X (3, 4)	
X (4, 2)	↓	X (4, 4)	↓

As long as the programmer is aware of this situation and knows what he is getting, everything is fine. Otherwise, it is best to play it safe and use dimensions in the subroutine (fixed or adjustable) which match those of a full array in the main program.

Summary of Rules for Subroutines

1. The subroutine name cannot appear anywhere in the subprogram except in its initial statement.

2. The arguments listed in a SUBROUTINE statement may include non-subscripted variables, array names, and names of other functions or subroutines. These are treated as dummy arguments in that they are replaced by actual arguments which are taken from a similar list supplied by each call to the subroutine.

3. None of the dummy arguments in a SUBROUTINE statement list may appear in an EQUIVALENCE, DATA, or EXTERNAL statement within the subroutine.

4. Control is given to a subroutine by means of a CALL statement whose list of actual arguments must agree in number, type, and sequence with the dummy list in the initial statement of that subroutine.

5. When arrays are used as dummy arguments, they must be dimensioned within the subroutine. Unless adjustable dimensions are used, the size of the dummy array must agree with that of the actual array specified in a call. If the dummy array is not dimensioned in the subroutine, only the first element will be available for use.

6. Dummy variables may be given any legitimate names, even those used for actual variables in the main program. The same holds true for statement numbers in a subroutine.

7. Actual arguments in a CALL statement list include constants, variables, array names, arithmetic expressions, and subprogram names. When a function subprogram name appears in such a list, its name must also appear in an EXTERNAL statement.

8. Any subroutine arguments which are to be used to return values to the main program must appear on the left side of an equal sign, in an input/output list, or as actual arguments in a CALL statement.

9. If subroutine A calls subroutine B, the subroutine B, while working under A's control, can't call subroutine A. (It can of course, RETURN to A or, for that matter, call subroutine C.)

The COMMON Statement

In Chapter VI (p. 162) we described the EQUIVALENCE statement as being a way in which the FORTRAN programmer can exercise some control over the use of a processor's memory. This control, as was seen by the discussion, is only nominal in that it allows the programmer to specify multiple names for a given location, but still limits his ability to locate a given variable relative to other variables. The COMMON statement supplies this capability.

Blank and Labeled Common

A list of variables appearing in a COMMON statement of the form

```
COMMON A, X, T, I, J, etc.
```

will be assigned sequential locations in memory. Each of the variables in this list may be subscripted or non-subscripted, but the subscripts must be constants. The area containing this sequence of variables is called a common block and is treated as a large unit by FORTRAN. There can be any number of such blocks in a program, and each may or may not be given a name. When a block is named by the programmer, this is called labeled common. When no name is given, the type of block is blank common. Blank common blocks are separated by double slashes, so that in the statement

```
COMMON A, Y, W//X, B, Z, T, I
```

the variables will be stored in the sequence listed, but A, Y and W will be treated as a unit separate from X, B, Z, T and I, which will constitute another unit. Usually, if the programmer wishes a certain list to be treated as a unit, he assigns some name to that list by using labeled common. The form is to assign the name as one would any variable name (type doesn't matter) and place that name ahead of the list, enclosed by slashes:

```
COMMON/TGTHER/X, B, EFFL, TOOT/SMACK/Y, Z, L
```

Based on the above statement, FORTRAN would store X, B, EFFL and TOOT in that order and assign the name TGTHER to that block. Similarly, a second block name SMACK would contain Y, Z and L in that order. A program may have more than one COMMON statement in it. The variables will be stored together in the sequence listed, beginning with the first variable listed in the earliest COMMON statement and continuing through the last variable listed in the last COMMON statement. Suppose we had the following situation:

```
COMMON B, DRUB, KNADEL/BLOB1/X, HY, LONG, Z//R, U
```

Other Statements

```
COMMON/BLOB2/N, SUBJ, B4J/BLOB1/SUMX, SUMY, SQRX//SIZE, TOP
```

FORTRAN arranges the COMMON storage as follows:

B	DRUB	KNADEL	R	U	SIZE	TOP

Blank Common

X	HY	LONG	Z	SUMX	SUMY	SQRX

BLOB1

N	SUBJ	B4J

BLOB2

The single statement

```
COMMON B, DRUB, KNADEL, R, U, SIZE, TOP/BLOB1/X, HY,
LONG, Z, SUMX, SUMY, SQRX/BLOB2/N, SUBJ, B4J
```

does the same thing.

Subscripted Variables in COMMON Statement

Lists in COMMON statements containing subscripted variables may be subject to size adjustment. This happens when the effects of COMMON and EQUIVALENCE statements are combined. For example, the sequence

```
DIMENSION G (4)
COMMON D, BJ4, C
EQUIVALENCE (C, G(2))
```

will force the common block D, BJ4, C to become

```
D, BJ4, C
   G(1), G(2). G(3), G(4)
```

Note that the common block may be extended forward but not backward. Thus we can't write something like

```
DIMENSION G (4)
COMMON D, BJ4, C
EQUIVALENCE (BJ4, G (4))
```

since this would force the beginning of the common block beyond D, its previously specified origin. In connection with this, it is illegal to equivalence two variables in the same or in different common blocks, just as it is illegal to equivalence two members of the same array.

COMMON Statements and Subprograms

The most useful property of the COMMON statement is that it can be used to link a main program with any number of subprograms. When COMMON statements appear in both a subprogram and the main program which calls that subprogram, it is not necessary to list those arguments in the SUBROUTINE or CALL statements. To illustrate, consider the sequence

```
REAL JMAX, NOISE, LGTH                     ┐
COMMON E, JMAX, NOISE, LGTH, B (25)        │ segment
                                           │ of main
[Other statements]                         │ program
                                           │
CALL IDENT                                 ┘

[More main program statements]
SUBROUTINE IDENT                           ┐
REAL J1, J2, J3                            │
COMMON GR, J1, J2, J3, Y (25)              │ subroutine
                                           │
[Processing]                               │
RETURN                                     │
END                                        ┘
```

What happens here is that the dummy arguments J1, J2, J3, GR and Y, by virtue of their appearance in a COMMON statement, will be linked with corresponding arguments in a COMMON statement in the main program. Thus, in this example the subroutine will use E, JMAX, NOISE, LGTH, and the array B wherever it refers to GR, J1, J2, J3 and Y, respectively. Various gimmicks are possible with the arrangement. For example, it is not necessary to use all of the listed arguments in a subroutine. So that if a common block is set up containing the sequence E, JMAX, NOISE, LGTH and B for use in one subroutine, and another subroutine requires only JMAX and LGTH, the second subroutine would still include a COMMON statement containing five arguments, but the actual routine would use only the second and fourth members of that list. Note also that the COMMON statement in the main program could be used to supply dimension information.

Special Considerations

For systems like the IBM 360 and RCA SPECTRA 70, where a varying number of locations may be assigned to a variable, special care must be taken when setting up common blocks. Let's consider the following:

```
COMPLEX * 16 G
REAL *8 F, BW*4                                  segment of main program
INTEGER*2 MINS
COMMON G, BW, MINS, F

COMPLEX* 16 W
REAL * 8 BG, S*4                                 segment of first subprogram
INTEGER*2 NTIX
COMMON W, S, NTIX, BG

REAL D, H, WDTH, HGT, LGTH*8                     segment of
INTEGER*2 AX, BAX, DAX                           second
COMMON LGTH, D, H, BAX,AX, DAX,HGT,WDTH          subprogram
```

These segments set up a common area with the following multiple assignments:

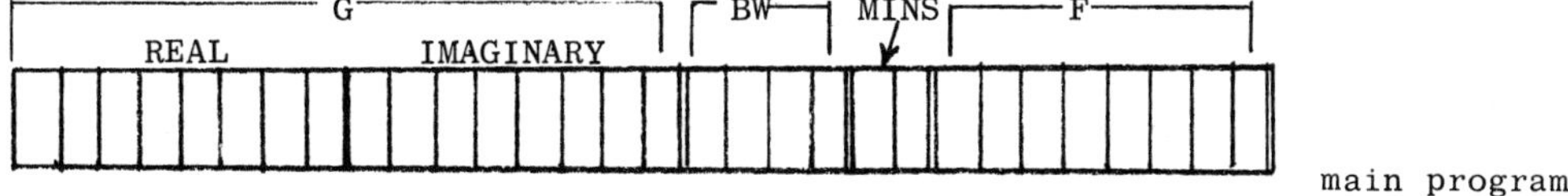

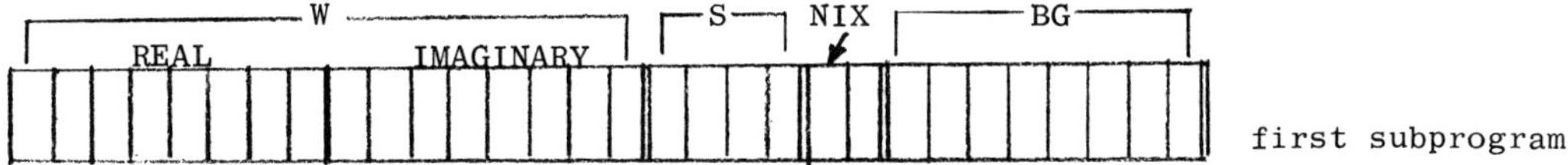

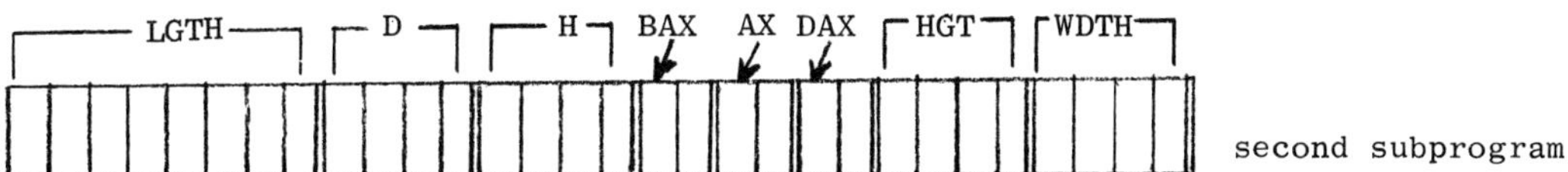

As a result, the variable LGTH would occupy the same storage as the real portion of W and G. Similarly the variables D and H would refer to the memory occupied by the imaginary portion of W or G. This is fine as long as the programmer keeps track of what's where and what type it is.

To help the bookkeeping in this regard, it is recommended that COMMON and EQUIVALENCE lists be organized by variable type using the following sequence.

Complex Double Precision

Complex

Double Precision

Real

Integer

Logical

Integer (shortened form)

Logical (shorthand form)

COMMON and DATA

In the previous chapter under the discussion of the DATA statement, it was pointed out that CDC 3600/3400/3200 FORTRAN uses a slightly different form for the DATA statement. We'll describe that here since it also allows the assignment of actual values to members of common blocks. The general form is

```
DATA (A = list), (B = list), etc.
```

where A and B are variable names and "list" is a sequence of constant values to be placed in the designated locations. Data may be placed in arrays in several ways: Each element can be separately designated, or parts of arrays may be assigned as follows:

```
DIMENSION R (4)
DATA ((R (I), I = 1, 4) = 7., 2., 6.4., 12.)
```

The only restriction in this implied DO-loop form is that the increment must always be 1. Repeating numbers may also be specified, using the following form:

```
DIMENSION R (10)
DATA ((R (I), I = 1, 10) = 7., 2., 8 (6.6))
```

Groups of constants may be repeated. For example, the sequence

```
DIMENSION R (12)
DATA ((R (I), I = 1, 12) = 4 (2., 3., 4.))
```

will place values 2., 3., 4., 2., 3., 4., 2., 3., 4., 2., 3., 4., in R (1) through R (12), respectively.

When used with logical arrays, the DATA statement in CDC FORTRAN stores logical constants (1 for .TRUE., 0 for .FALSE.) in groups of 32. If the number of elements in an array is not a multiple of 32, the remainder is filled with zeros. For example, suppose we had a two dimensional array of 12 logical elements called TOC (dimensions 3 x 4) with values as follows:

Row \ Col.	1	2	3	4
1	T	T	T	F
2	F	T	F	T
3	T	F	F	F

Since these elements would be stored by column, the sequence in memory would be

TFTTTFTFFFTF

and, in terms of 1's and 0's, the sequence would be

101110100010

The DATA statement accepts this information as an octal constant. The conversion, then, is

101	110	100	010
5	6	4	2

Adding the necessary zeros, we get an octal constant of 56420000000 and the DATA statement form would be

```
DATA (TOC = 56420000000B)
```

When used with COMMON statements, it is possible to do the following:

```
COMMON/GROUP1/X(4), Y(4)
DATA (X = 1., 4(7.), 3(6.4)
```

FORTRAN will go ahead and place 1. in X (1), 7. in X (2) through X (4), 7. in Y (1) and 6.4 in Y (2), Y (3), and Y (4).

The BLOCK DATA Subprogram

Compilers other than the CDC 3600/3400/3200 versions supply a BLOCK DATA statement for entering data into common blocks. It is required that this be used as the first statement of a subprogram which specifies the common block and gives the initial values. Let's go back to a previous example in which we had a common block containing a complex double precision variable G, double precision variable F, single precision variable BW and half size integer MINS. Suppose we wanted the following initial values stored.

G = 13.76774295 + 7.06642897 i

F = 124.611279844

BW = 0.6453

MINS = 7

Our BLOCK DATA subprogram would look as follows:

```
BLOCK DATA
COMMON G, BW, MINS, F
COMPLEX * 16 G/(13.76774295, 7.06642897)/
REAL BW/0.6453/, F * 8/124.611279844/
INTEGER * 2 MINS/7/
END
```

This type of subprogram just appears with the main program; it is not called. Only non-executable statements may be included. Furthermore, the entire common block must be listed in the COMMON statement, even though it may not be desired to provide initial values for all of the list's members. (The IBM 1401, 1410, 1440, 1460, 7040/44/90/94 FORTRAN compilers do not provide the BLOCK DATA statement).

APPENDIX A

Representation of Information in a Computer's Memory

In Chapter I it was indicated that the memory of a digital computer is composed of a large number of a very small magnetic elements (bits) which are designed to operate in one of two distinct modes (bistable elements). Physically, these two modes represent full magnetization in one direction or full magnetization in the other direction. For purposes of reference and discussion, it is more convenient to consider these two modes as "yes" or "no," "on" or "off," or 1 or 0. With this arrangement, it is possible to design the logical circuitry so that each legal character is represented by a fixed number of bits being turned "on" or "off" in a unique combination. If we use the symbolic notation of 1 for the "on" status and 0 for the "off" status, then combinations of these 1's and 0's represent numbers in a system where the operating base is 2. This binary number system is completely analogous to our standard decimal base with regard to the construction of the numerical values. The three digit number 110, for example, implies in the decimal system:

$$1 \times 10^2 + 1 \times 10^1 + 0 \times 10^0 = 100 + 10 + 0$$

and in the binary system:

$$1 \times 2^2 + 1 \times 2^1 + 0 \times 2^0 = 4 + 2 + 0$$

Since only two digits exist in the binary system, all numbers and characters are built up by a succession of these digits. So 0 is represented by 0, 1 is represented by 1, 2 by 10, 3 by 11, 9 by 1001 and so on. Today's digital computers use two basic standards for representing information. Most present models use a system wherein each legal character is represented by a unit of six bits (referred to as a six bit byte). More recent types of computers (such as the IBM 360 and RCA SPECTRA 70) use an eight bit byte. These two methods of representing data are summarized in Tables A1 and A2. Although not shown in these tables, it should be noted that each byte in the memory of a computer is augmented by an extra bit (so that the six bit byte, for example, is really composed of seven bits). This extra bit is called a check bit and is used for internal circuit checking.

In many digital computers, a number of bytes are linked together by the logical circuitry to form a word. This word can be used to store a number of individual characters of information or can be used as a single unit to store one numerical quantity. When the latter is the case, that quantity, expressed as a binary number, occupies the entire word. Thus, for example, in the CDC 3600, which uses a word length of 48 bits, a single value may be composed of a combination of 48 1's and 0's. Since dealing directly with binary numbers is awkward when done manually, the programmer wishing to represent these quantities uses the octal system. Since 8, the base of the octal system, is 2 raised to the third power, each group of three binary digits may be represented by a single octal digit. Thus, for example, if we were dealing with a computer whose word length was 12 bits, the decimal quantity 110 would be represented as

$$1 \times 64 + 1 \times 32 + 0 \times 16 + 1 \times 8 + 1 \times 4 + 1 \times 2 + 0 \times 1$$

or

000001101110

Dividing this into groups of three, we can see that the octal equivalent of this quantity is:

$$\underbrace{000}_{0}\ \underbrace{001}_{1}\ \underbrace{101}_{5}\ \underbrace{110}_{6} \quad = \quad 156_8 = 0 \times 8^3 + 1 \times 8^2 + 5 \times 8^1 + 6 \times 8^0$$

Table A1
Source Program Characters
Six Bit Byte -
(All bits "on" represented as 6-5-4-4-3-2-1)

Character	How Punched*	How Stored	Character	How Punched	How Stored	Character	How Punched	How Stored
Blank		6-5-4-3	J	11-1	5-1	'	8-4	4-3
0	0	4-2	K	11-2	5-2	(	0-8-4	6-4-3
1	1	1	L	11-3	5-2-1	)	12-8-4	6-5-4-3
2	2	2	M	11-4	5-3	$	11-8-3	5-4-2-1
3	3	2-1	N	11-5	5-3-1	*	11-8-4	5-4-2
4	4	3	O	11-6	5-3-2			
5	5	3-1	P	11-7	5-3-2-1	/	0-1	6-1
6	6	3-2	Q	11-8	5-4	[	12-8-5	6-5-4-3-1
7	7	3-2-1	R	11-9	5-4-1	<	12-8-6	6-5-4-3-2
8	8	4	S	0-2	6-2	≢	12-8-7	6-5-4-3-2-1
9	9	4-1	T	0-3	6-2-1	]	11-8-5	5-4-3-1
			U	0-4	6-3	;	11-8-6	5-4-3-2
A	12-1	6-5-1	V	0-5	6-3-1			
B	12-2	6-5-2	W	0-6	6-3-2	\	0-8-6	6-5-3-2
C	12-3	6-5-2-1	X	0-7	6-3-2-1			
D	12-4	6-5-3	Y	0-8	6-4			
E	12-5	6-5-3-1	Z	0-9	6-4-1	:	8-5	4-3-1
F	12-6	6-5-3-2	+	12	6	>	8-6	4-3-2
G	12-7	6-5-3-2-1	-	11	5	√	8-7	4-3-2-1
H	12-8	6-5-4	=	8-3	4-2-1			
I	12-9	6-5-4-1	.	12-8-3	6-5-4-2-1			
?	12-0	6-5-4-2	,	0-8-3	5-4-2-1			

*See Figure 1

Table A2
Source Program Characters
Eight Bit Byte*
(All bits "on" represented as 8-7-6-5-4-3-2-1)

Character	How Punched	How Stored	Character	How Punched	How Stored	Character	How Punched	How Stored
Blank		7	J	11-1	8-6-4-2	'	8-4	7-3-2-1
0	0	7-5	K	11-2	8-6-4-2-1	(	0-8-4	7-4
1	1	7-5-1	L	11-3	8-6-4-3	)	12-8-4	7-4-1
2	2	7-5-2	M	11-4	8-6-4-3-1	$	11-8-3	7-3
3	3	7-5-2-1	N	11-5	8-6-4-3-2	*	11-8-4	7-4-2
4	4	7-5-3	O	11-6	8-6-4-3-2-1	/	0-1	7-4-3-2-1
5	5	7-5-3-1	P	11-7	8-6-5	[	12-8-5	8-6-5-4-2-1
6	6	7-5-3-2	Q	11-8	8-6-5-1	≤	12-8-6	7-5-4-3
7	7	7-5-3-2-1	R	11-9	8-6-5-2	≢	12-8-7	5-3-2-1
8	8	7-5-4	S	0-2	8-6-5-2-1	]	11-8-5	8-6-5-4-3-1
9	9	7-5-4-1	T	0-3	8-6-5-3	;	11-8-6	7-5-4-2-1
A	12-1	8-6-1	U	0-4	8-6-5-3-1	\	0-8-6	8-6-5-4-3
B	12-2	8-6-2	V	0-5	8-6-5-3-2	:	8-5	7-5-4-2
C	12-3	8-6-2-1	W	0-6	8-6-5-3-2-1	>	8-6	7-5-4-3-2
D	12-4	8-6-3	X	0-7	8-6-5-4	√	8-7	5-3
E	12-5	8-6-3-1	Y	0-8	8-6-5-4-1			
F	12-6	8-6-3-2	Z	0-9	8-6-5-4-2			
G	12-7	8-6-3-2-1	+	12	7-4-2-1			
H	12-8	8-6-4	-	11	7-4-3-1			
I	12-9	8-6-4-1	=	8-3	7-5-4-3-1			
?	12-0	7-6-4-3-3-1	.	12-8-3	7-4-3-2			
			,	0-8-3	7-4-3			

* Additional symbols are available in this system (e.g., lower case letters # , %, !, etc.).

APPENDIX B

Magnetic Tape

Magnetic tape used for data processing is of the same general type (but much higher quality) as that used for audio recording and playback. Each single digit of data is stored as a series of seven magnetic impules across the width of the tape (usually 1/2"). (Most recent systems, like the IBM 360 and RCA SPECTRA 70, use 1/2" tape with 9 tracks.) This method of storage is extremely compact. Present-day tape units (drives) are capable of placing hundreds of digits of information on a single inch of tape. Three densities are generally available: 200, 556 and 800 characters per inch. Thus the data punched on an 80-column card can be represented on a length of tape amounting to roughly 1/7". Since the standard 10-inch diameter reel contains 2400 feet of tape, one can see that a single reel of tape can accommodate one hell of a lot of data.

The coding of data on magnetic tape is made to be compatible with the computer accepting the data and can be represented as a series of magnetic impulses across the tape width. There are seven or nine channels across the tape; six or eight of these are used for symbol representation and the other one is used for internal checking. (See Appendix A.) The picture given below schematically depicts the representation of characters on binary coded decimal (BCD) seven channel tape. In this case the seventh channel adds a bit to all characters having an odd number of bits.

Schematic Representation of Data on Seven Track Magnetic Tape

*A magnetic impulse is generated in this channel so that all characters are represented by an even number of impulses (even parity).

The logical unit for data recorded on magnetic tape is the <u>record</u>. A record may be 80 columns long (the equivalent of one punched card), or can be shorter or longer, the length being determined by the computer program which transcribes the data onto tape. Tape systems are designed to skip a length of tape between records automatically (3/4" for 7-channel tape; 0.6" for 9-channel tape). This is called the <u>inter-record gap</u>. The standard record length is equivalent to that containing the information from an 80-column card and as such is called a <u>card image</u> and many programs are designed specifically to read data from tape as card images. For purposes of data storage, however, it can be seen that the card image is an uneconomical record length. Let's examine this further. Suppose we are to record a card image on seven channel tape at the most frequently used density, i.e., 556 characters per inch. Thus our 80 columns of data (including blanks) will occupy 80/556 or roughly 1/7 inch of tape length. At the end of this record, 3/4 inch of tape will be left blank and the next record then would be written. Thus our tape might be schematically represented as follows:

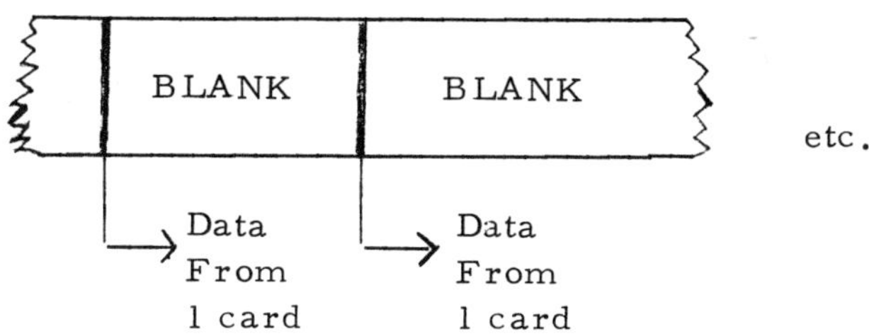

As a result, roughly 5/6 of the tape length is not being used for data but serves, rather, to separate data. This situation is avoided by programming the transcription of data onto tape such that several cards are run together to form one record. This process, known as blocking, provides taped information which can be represented as follows:

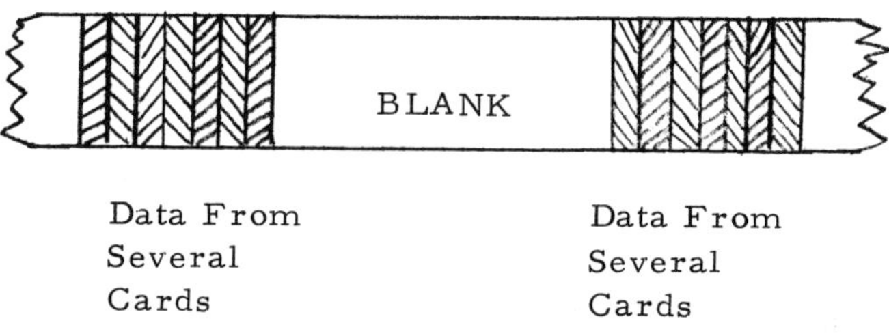

By using blocking programs, data are compressed into multicard records for compact storage. When data from a particular project are to be processed, the data are transcribed from the compressed (blocked) storage tape via a deblocking program to a data file tape containing card images. This data file usually serves as input to the processing programs. In many cases the processing program will include a deblocking routine within its structure. When a computer is instructed to read information from tape it will read one record each time the instruction is executed.

That is, it will stop reading when an inter-record gap is encountered. Similarly, when an instruction is given to write on tape, an inter-record gap is automatically added immediately after the information is written. Consequently, the following information must always appear in read or write statements involving tape:

1. The tape unit to be used must be identified (unit number).

2. Where in storage the information is coming from (or going to). This also defines the length of the record. To exploit the advantages of blocking information, data from various projects are usually stored on the same reel of tape. Since all inter-record gaps are the same, some special way must be provided to distinguish between data files. The signal used for this purpose is the end-of-file indicator or <u>tape mark</u>. This is generated automatically after the last record of a file is written and can then be used as a test signal for a program to take some prescribed course of action. For example, a program could be instructed to read and store data until the tape mark is reached, at which point calculations are to be performed.

When transmitting several data files to a common reel of tape some identifying information is usually included as a separate record directly in front of each file (<u>file header label</u>). Similarly it is often desirable to make the last record of a file an identifying record (<u>file trailer label</u>) containing the number of records in the file, as well as the total number of cards. (Note: these are identical only if the data are stored as card images. Otherwise there will be fewer records than there were cards, the ratio depending on how many cards were blocked together (<u>blocking factor</u>).)

Another tape-handling capability is one which allows the computer, via program instructions, to backspace a record. This is used to handle tape error conditions which for a variety of reasons, prevented the reading or writing of informations from or onto tape. If such a condition is encountered, programs usually include a small routine which causes the record to be backspaced and the read or write is reattempted. If the Nth attempt is unsuccessful (some people use an N of 10, others go up to 100) the attempts are terminated. In the case of a write, instructions are usually given to skip over some blank tape and try again. When a read has been attempted unsuccessfully N times, the usual procedure is to call for a halt (PAUSE) and the printing of an error message so that the programmer or machine operator can decide what to do.

It is also possible to instruct the computer to rewind a reel. This causes a series of backspaces until the beginning of the first record is sensed. This location is known as the <u>load point</u> and is indicated by the presence of a thin reflective strip which the tape unit is designed to sense.

FORTRAN IV provides several instructions for manipulations and transmitting information to and from tape. First we'll handle straight reading and writing. As previously indicated, the general form

READ (L, M) list

or

WRITE (L, M) list.

still applies, thus implying that instead of dealing with an input card or a printed line, we now deal with a card image or, as it were, a line image. Line images produced on an output tape are printed at some appropriate time, using a print program. L does not refer to a tape unit but, rather, to a logical unit number which sends FORTRAN scurrying to a table somewhere in memory. From this table is obtained the tape unit number to be used.

The tape unit number is set by hand on a dial at the top of the tape unit. Thus, for example, if logical unit 1 referred to tape drive no. 5, the statements

```
      READ (1, 14) X, Y, Z
14    FORMAT (3X, F4.1, 4X, F5.0, 2X, F6.2)
```

will cause the reading of a single card image record from tape unit 5, with the storage of three quantities in X, Y and Z, respectively, according to the specifications in FORMAT statement no. 14.

End-of-file Statement

This statement takes the general form

END FILE N

where N is the unit number. When executed, this statement will close the file on unit N with a tape mark.

The REWIND Statement

This statement is written as

REWIND N

where N is the unit number. This statement includes in it the activity generated in the END FILE statement. Thus, it will end the file, then rewind the tape to the load point.

The BACKSPACE Statement

The statement

BACKSPACE N

will cause unit N to be backspaced one record.

As in the case of audio tape systems, when information is written on digital tape, any information that was previously there is automatically erased. To prevent accidental erasure of information, the tape reels are equipped with removable plastic rings (file protect rings). When a file protect ring is removed from a reel it becomes impossible to write on that tape, thus permitting only reading. If the program should come to an instruction telling it to write on unit 6, for example, and unit 6 contained a reel without its file protect ring, the machine would find it impossible to continue executing the program.

APPENDIX C

Summary of FORTRAN IV Source Statements

The following table lists the source statements available in FORTRAN IV, together with comments about their use. For purposes of illustration the following nomenclature is used.

X is a single precision real variable

D is a double precision variable

C is a complex variable

Z is any legitimate arithmetic expression in floating point mode

H is any legitimate arithmetic expression containing complex quantities

K is an integer (fixed point) variable

J is any legitimate arithmetic expression in fixed point mode

G is a logical variable

E is any legitimate logical expression

N is a statement number

I is a counter

M is a subscript

S represents a statement (<u>not</u> a statement number)

F represents the name of a subprogram

A represents a floating point constant

L represents a fixed point constant

Statement	Where program goes after encountering this statement	Executable or Non-Executable	Remarks	Not Available On
X = Z K = J X = J K = Z G = E	Next statement in sequence	Executable	May be placed anywhere in the program.	
D = Z	Next statement in sequence	Executable	May be placed anywhere in the program.	RCA 3301, IBM 1401/1410/1440/1460, UNIVAC III
C = H	Next statement in sequence	Executable	May be placed anywhere in the program.	RCA 3301, IBM 1401/1410/1440/1460, UNIVAC III
ASSIGN N TO K	Next statement in sequence	Executable	May be placed anywhere in the program.	IBM 1401/1410/1440/1460
BACKSPACE I	Next statement in sequence	Executable	May be placed anywhere in the program	
BLOCK DATA	Next statement in sequence	Non-Executable	Must be the first statement of a subprogram which contains no executable statements. This subprogram places initial values in labeled common blocks.	IBM 1401, 1410, 1440 and 1460. IBM 7040/44/90/94 and CDC 3600/3400/3200 use DATA statement

Statement	Where program goes after encountering this statement	Executable or Non-Executable	Remarks	Not Available On
CALL F ( )	First statement in subprogram F	Executable	May be placed anywhere in the program.	
COMMON	Next statement in sequence	Non-Executable	Cannot be the last statement in a DO loop. Otherwise, it may appear anywhere in a program.	
COMPLEX C	Next statement in sequence	Non-Executable	Cannot end a DO loop and must appear in the program before any other mention of the variables in the list.	RCA 3301, IBM 1401/1410/1440/1460, UNIVAC III
CONTINUE	Next statement in sequence	Executable	May be placed anywhere but finds most frequent use as the last statement in a DO loop.	
DATA X, K/A, L/	Next statement in sequence	Non-Executable	Cannot be used to initialize values in unlabeled (blank) COMMON.	IBM 1401/1410/1440/1460
DIMENSION X (L, L, L)	Next statement in sequence	Non-Executable	This cannot be the last statement in a DO loop and must appear before any other mention of variable X in the program.	

Statement	Where program goes after encountering this statement	Executable or Non-Executable	Remarks	Not Available On
DO N I = I, M, L	Next statement in the DO loop, until the loop is executed the required number of times, after which time the program continues.	Executable	This cannot be the last statement in a DO loop.	
DOUBLE PRECISION D	Next statement in sequence	Non-Executable	Cannot end a DO loop and must appear in the program before any other mention of the variables in the list.	RCA 3301, IBM 1401, IBM 1410/1440/1460, UNIVAC III
END	Ends compilation of a program	Executable	This must be the last physical statement in the source main program or source subprogram.	
END FILE L	Next statement in sequence	Executable	May be placed anywhere in a program.	
ENTRY F ( )	To the entry point in the subprogram specified by name F.	Executable	May be placed anywhere in the program	RCA 3301, PHILCO 2000, IBM 1401/1410/1440/1460, IBM 7040/44/90/94, UNIVAC III, UNIVAC 1107

Statement	Where program goes after encountering this statement	Executable or Non-Executable	Remarks	Not Available On
EQUIVALENCE ( )	Next statement in sequence	Non-Executable	This cannot be the last statement in a DO loop.	
FORMAT ( )	Next statement after input-output statement in which reference to the FORMAT statement was made.	Non-Executable	This statement may not be used to end a DO loop.	
FUNCTION F ( )	Next statement in sequence	Non-Executable	This statement can only be used as the first statement of a FUNCTION subprogram.	
GO TO N	Statement N	Executable	May not be used as the last statement of a DO loop.	
GO TO K, (N_1, N_2, N_m)	Statement number last assigned to K	Executable	Used with ASSIGN statement. May not be used as the last statement of a DO loop.	IBM 1401/1410/1440/1460
GO TO (N_1, N_2, N_m), I	The Ith statement number in the parenthetical list.	Executable	May not be used as the last statement of a DO loop.	
IF (Z) N_1, N_2, N_3 (also IF (J) N_1, N_2, N_3)	N_1 if $Z < 0$. N_2 if $Z = 0$. N_3 if $Z > 0$.	Executable	May not be used as the last statement of a DO loop.	

Statement	Where program goes after encountering this statement	Executable or Non-Executable	Remarks	Not Available On
IF (E) S	If (E) is true, statement S is executed, and normal sequence follows. If (E) is false S is skipped.	Executable	May be placed anywhere but should not end a DO loop.	
IF (E) N_1, N_2	If (E) is true, the program goes to statement no. N_1. Otherwise, it goes to N_2.	Executable	Cannot end a DO	IBM 360, RCA SPECTRA 70, PHILCO 2000, RCA 3301, IBM 1401/1410/1440/1460, IBM 7040/44/90/94, UNIVAC III, 1107.
INTEGER K	Next statement in sequence	Non-Executable	Cannot end a DO loop and must appear in the program before any other mention of the variables in the list.	
LOGICAL G	Next statement in sequence	Non-Executable	Cannot end a DO loop and must appear in the program before any other mention of the variables in the list.	IBM 1401
NAMELIST/X/D, C, G	Next statement in sequence	Non-Executable	Must be placed ahead of first usage.	Available only on IBM 360, RCA SPECTRA 70 and GE 625/635

Statement	Where program goes after encountering this statement	Executable or Non-Executable	Remarks	Not Available On
PAUSE L	Next statement in sequence	Executable	May be placed anywhere.	
READ (L, N) X, K, G	Next statement in sequence	Executable	May be placed anywhere.	
REAL X	Next statement	Non-Executable	May not end a DO loop and must appear in a program before any other mention of the variable in the list.	
RETURN	The first statement in the main program following the reference to the subprogram	Executable	Must be the last statement in any subprogram.	
RETURN I	The Ith statement number given in a list of arguments in a CALL to the subprogram.	Executable	May be placed anywhere in a subprogram.	Available only on IBM 360
REWIND I	Next statement	Executable	May be placed anywhere in the program. Causes end-of-file mark to be written before it rewinds.	
STOP	This terminates the execution of a program.	Executable	Should be placed where a final halt is desired.	

Statement	Where program goes after encountering this statement	Executable or Non-Executable	Remarks	Not Available On
SUBROUTINE F ( )	Next statement in sequence	Non-Executable	Must be the first statement in a subroutine sub-program.	
WRITE (L, N) X, K, G	Next statement in sequence	Executable	May be placed anywhere	

APPENDIX D

Machine Indicators

In Chapter IV we discussed programming techniques whereby we were able to direct the sequence of instructions along one of several alternate pathways depending on conditions resulting from input or calculated interim results. For example, the IF statement allows us to skip a statement under certain conditions, the GO TO statements enable us to bypass entire groups of instructions, or to return to a set of previously executed instructions, etc. All of these techniques operate on situations resulting from computed internal conditions using decision criteria set up by the programmer as part of his program.

There are additional provisions for altering the course of a program which depend on features built into the circuitry of the processor. These features, termed machine indicators, are treated by FORTRAN as on-off switches whose status determines the instruction sequence to be followed. In some processors, these indicators actually exist as hardware. In others, they are simulated by subprograms included as part of the FORTRAN compiler. When the former is true, it is possible for the machine operator to control the status of some of these indicators externally at any time during the execution of the program.

Sense Switch Indicators

Many processors (including the IBM 7040/44/90/94 and CDC 3600/3400/3200), are equipped with a series of physical switches (6 is the standard number) which may be turned on or off at any time. The status test for these switches takes the following general form:

CALL SSWTCH (I, J)

Where I is an integer constant or variable denoting the switch number to be tested. J is another variable set aside by the programmer for use of the testing routine. If sense switch I is on, FORTRAN will place a 1 in location J. If sense switch I is off, FORTRAN will place a 2 in location J. It is then up to the programmer to use the value of J in a subsequent IF statement, or however it suits his purpose.

The sense switch testing routine in CDC 3600/3400/3200 FORTRAN requires no call statement. Instead, it is set up so that the test can be performed by means of the following IF statement:

IF (SENSE SWITCH I) N1, N2

Where I is the sense switch number. If sense switch I is on, the program transfers to statement number N1. If it is off, the program goes to statement N2. (Sense switch tests are also available in RCA 3301, UNIVAC III, and PHILCO 2000 FORTRAN, but as routines which simulate the existence of actual sense switches. In the case of the PHILCO 2000, up to 48 different sense switches may be tested).

Sense Light Indicators

These indicators are turned on or off by the programmer using special statements. Other statements are then available for testing the status of these indicators. For setting a sense light, the following statement is used:

CALL SLITE (I)

Where I is an integer constant ranging from zero to four (except for the UNIVAC III, which allows a maximum I of 8, and the PHILCO 2000, which allows a maximum I of 48). If I is zero, FORTRAN will turn all of the sense lights off. Otherwise, it will turn the Ith sense light on.

This statement is used in conjunction with a test statement of the form:

```
CALL SLITET (I, J)
```

Where I is an integer constant corresponding to the sense light number, and J is an integer variable reserved by the programmer for this use. If sense light I is on, J is set to 1 and FORTRAN turns the light off; if the light is already off, J is set to a value of 2. (IBM 1401/1440/1460 FORTRAN does not have the sense light feature).

In CDC 3600/3400/3200 FORTRAN, the sense light set and test statements take the following form:

```
SENSE LIGHT I
IF (SENSE LIGHT I) N1, N2
```

Where I is the sense light number. In the first statement, if I equals zero, all lights are turned off. Otherwise the Ith light is turned on. In the second statement, if sense light I is on, the program goes to statement number N1; otherwise it goes to statement number N2.

Overflow Test

In Chapter I we discussed maximum and minimum limits on numerical values in various processors. In many cases it is possible to include checks in a program whereby violations of these limits are detected and appropriate action taken. The general form for such a test is

```
CALL OVERFL (J)
```

Where J is an integer variable set up by the programmer. This type of test is usually inserted in a program immediately after a computation takes place where a possible violation of limits is anticipated. If an overflow occurs (a floating number beyond the maximum limit is computed) a value of 1 is placed in J. If no overflow exists, J is set to a value of 2. If an overflow exists (a value is calculated below the allowable minimum) a value of 3 is placed in J. (In some processors such as the PHILCO 2000 and UNIVAC III, no action is taken on an overflow, i.e., the value of 3 for J is not used).

As in other indicator tests, the CDC 3600/3400/3200 version uses the IF statement in the form

```
IF OVERFLOW FAULT N1, N2
```

This statement checks for an overflow as the result of an addition or subtraction. If such a condition exists, the overflow indicator is turned off and the program goes to statement N1. Otherwise, a transfer is made to statement N2. Another statement is provided which takes the form:

IF EXPONENT FAULT N1, N2

All overflows are handled by this statement. If an overflow occurs, the indicator is turned off and the program goes to statement N1. Otherwise, the program transfers to statement N2. If an overflow occurs, the value being tested is set to zero and the program reacts as if the indicator were turned off.

Divide Check Tests

In a complex program where values are changing continually, it may sometimes happen that a combination of values is produced whereby the program is asked to divide a quantity by zero. FORTRAN makes it possible to check for such a condition and take appropriate action if the condition should occur. The general form for this test is as follows:

CALL DVCHK (J)

If the program is being asked to divide by zero, a value of 1 is placed in location J and the indicator is turned off. Otherwise, a value of 2 is placed in J. Again, the IF statement form is used in CDC 3600/3400/3200 FORTRAN:

IF DIVIDE CHECK N1, N2

APPENDIX E

A Sample Program

A sample program is worked out in detail to indicate the steps in building up the sequence of instructions. A word length of 6 characters is assumed.

Means and Standard Deviations

It is desired to write a program which will summarize data in term of means and standard deviations. If we assign the name X to a given reading and there are N readings, then

$$\text{The mean for the X's} = X = \frac{\Sigma X}{N}$$

$$\text{The variance} = S_X^2 = \frac{\Sigma X^2 - \frac{(\Sigma X)^2}{N}}{N - 1}$$

$$\text{The standard deviation} = S_X = \sqrt{S_X^2}$$

$$\text{The standard error} = \frac{S_X}{\sqrt{N}}$$

Let's assume that each data card contains a set of single readings for each of the variables to be summarized and that our format will change with each run. Furthermore, we want our output sheet to look like this:

Label Information
Label Information
etc.
etc.

Data Summary

Var. Name   No.   Mean   Variance   Std. Dev.   Std. Error

Before we begin the actual programming it will behoove us to set up some general rules regarding the program. These, of course, are not hard and fast, but serve instead as conveniences for this program.

If one chooses to write the program differently, other conventions may be more suitable.

A. The last card to be printed at the top of the output sheet will contain 700007 in columns 1-6 as a signal that it is the last label card and no more will follow. Label cards will contain information in columns 7-72.

B. Variable names will be read in as input, one name to a card. Up to 12 characters (including spaces) will be allowed for variable names. (Columns 1-12).

C. Data will come in with a variable format. Following the last data card will be a special card having 100001 in columns 73-80 to indicate that all the data for a given run have been entered. 200002 in those columns will indicate that the last run of a series of runs has been entered.

D. Now we can set some limits. Let's say that we will handle up to 60 variables. That means we need the following arrays: 120 words for variable names (2 words per name), 60 words for counting the number of readings, 60 words for sums, 60 words for means, 60 words for storing each reading as it comes in, 60 words for variances, 60 words for standard deviations and 60 words for standard errors.

E. One more thing: The card preceding the first data card will contain the number of variables to be processed for the given run. We'll call this number NVAR. (This type of card is called a control card).

F. Now we'll prepare a block diagram for the program so that the logical sequence can be checked.

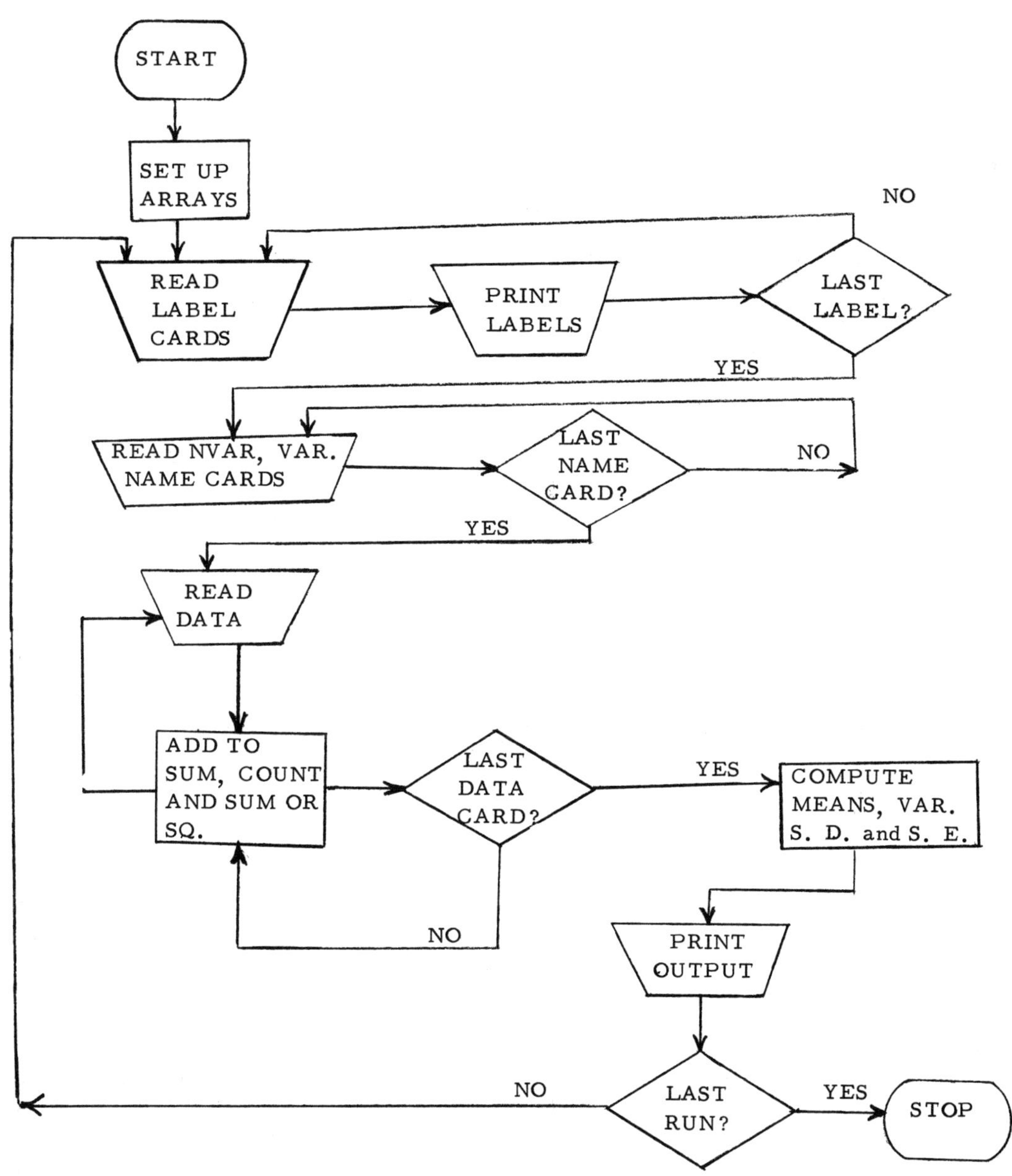
START
SET UP ARRAYS
READ LABEL CARDS
PRINT LABELS
LAST LABEL?
NO
YES
READ NVAR, VAR. NAME CARDS
LAST NAME CARD?
NO
YES
READ DATA
ADD TO SUM, COUNT AND SUM OR SQ.
LAST DATA CARD?
YES
NO
COMPUTE MEANS, VAR. S. D. and S. E.
PRINT OUTPUT
LAST RUN?
NO
YES
STOP

G. Output Format

According to our output requirements we shall be printing six types of data: variable names, no. of readings, means, variance, standard deviations, and standard error. Let's assign numbers of characters to these categories:

Variable names will occupy 12 spaces each.

We'll allow 5 digits for number of readings.

Means will be given in the form XXXXXX. XXXXXX.

Variance will be given in the form XXXXXXXX. XXXXXX.

Standard deviations will be given in the form XXXXXX. XXXXXX.

Standard errors will be given in the form XXXXXX. XXXXXX.

Hence the total number of occupied columns will be 12 + 5 + 14 + 16 + 14 + 14 or 75. This leaves 56 columns for spacing. Hence, 8 columns at the beginning of the page (plus one for carriage control) and 8 columns between variables will handle the spacing requirements. Thus our output FORMAT statement will say

```
FORMAT (9X, 2A6, 8X, F5.0, 8X, F14.6, 8X, F16.6, 8X, F14.6, 8X, F14
```

H. Variable Names

We'll name our arrays here and now so that no ambiguity will exist.

Variable names	VARNAM1 and VARNM2 (two-word variable name
Count fields	RDGS
Sum fields	SUM
Means	VRMEAN

Sum of squares	SUMSQR
Variance	VARNCE
Standard Deviation	STDDEV
Standard Error	STDERR
Individual Value	XVAL

The program, with comments, appears starting at the top of the next page and sample output is shown on page 239. Once the program and its structure are thoroughly understood, we can go back to our block diagram and fill in some additional details. This is shown on page 240.

```
CFIRST WE SHALL MAKE SURE THAT WE START AT THE TOP OF A PAGE.
 840  WRITE(6,3)
    3 FORMAT(1H1)
CTHEN WE SHALL SET UP OUR ARRAYS, AND READ AND PRINT LABEL CARDS.
      DIMENSION RDGS(60),SUM(60),VRMEAN(60),SUMSQR(60),VARNCE(60),STDDEV
     1(60),STDERR(60),XVAL(60),XLABEL(11),DATFMT(12),VARNM1(60),VARNM2(6
     20)
CWE FIRST HAVE A DO LOOP WHICH INITIALIZES ALL OF OUR ARRAYS.
    5 DO 30 I=1,NVAR
      RDGS(I)=0.
      SUM(I)=0.
      SUMSQR(I)=0.
      VRMEAN(I)=0.
      VARNCE(I)=0.
      STCCER(I)=0.
      STDERR(I)=0.
   30 CONTINUE
    2 READ(5,6)NSIGNL,XLABEL
    6 FORMAT(I6,11A6)
      WRITE(6,8)XLABEL
    8 FORMAT(33X,11A6)
CHERE WE SHALL TEST FOR LAST LABEL CARD AND READ THE NO. OF VARIABLES.
      IF(NSIGNL.NE.700007)GO TO 2
CNEXT WE SKIP THREE LINES TO SEPARATE THE HEADINGS FROM THE RESULTS
      WRITE(6,9)
    9 FORMAT(1H-)
   10 READ(5,12)NVAR
   12 FORMAT(I2)
CNOW THE VARIABLE NAMES, DATA FORMAT, FOLLOWED BY THE DATA.
      READ(5,15)(VARNM1(I),VARNM2(I),I=1,NVAR)
   15 FORMAT(2A6)
      READ(5,18)DATFMT
   18 FORMAT(12A6)
   20 READ(5,DATFMT)(XVAL(I),I=1,NVAR),NSIGNL
CNOTE THAT THIS CAUSES ONLY ONE CARD TO BE READ.
CAFTER A CHECK FOR LAST CARD WE WILL DO OUR PRELIMINARY CALCULATIONS.
      IF(NSIGNL.EQ.100001.OR.NSIGNL.EQ.200002)GO TO 200
      DO 40 I=1,NVAR
      RDGS(I)=RDGS(I)+1.0
      SUM(I)=SUM(I)+XVAL(I)
      SUMSQR(I)=SUMSQR(I)+XVAL(I)**2
   40 CONTINUE
CTHIS GETS US TO THE POINT WHERE WE ARE READY TO READ THE NEXT CARD.
      GO TO 20
CHERE WE SHALL PRINT HEADINGS AND THEN DO THE SUMMARY CALCULATIONS.
  200 WRITE(6,204)
  204 FORMAT(60X,12HDATA SUMMARY//)
  208 WRITE(6,212)
  212 FORMAT(18X,9HVAR. NAME,8X,3HNO.,12X,4HMEAN,14X,8HVARIANCE,9X,9HSTD
     1. DEV.,6X,10HSTD. ERROR//)
      DO 250 I=1,NVAR
      VRMEAN(I)=SUM(I)/RDGS(I)
      VARNCE(I)=(SUMSQR(I)-(VRMEAN(I)*SUM(I)))/(RDGS-1.0)
      STDDEV(I)=SQRT(VARNCE(I))
      STDERR(I)=STDDEV(I)/SQRT(RDGS)
      WRITE(6,230)VARNM1(I),VARNM2(I),RDGS(I),VRMEAN(I),VARNCE(I),STDDEV
     1(I),STDERR(I)
  230 FORMAT(17X,2A6,5X,F5.0,5X,F14.6,3X,F16.6,3X,F14.6,3X,F14.6)
  250 CONTINUE
      IF(NSIGNL.EQ.200002)STOP
      GO TO 5
      END
```

MEANS AND STANDARD DEVIATIONS PROGRAM
SAMPLE RUN
SPECIAL DATA

DATA SUMMARY

VAR. NAME	NO.	MEAN	VARIANCE	STD. DEV.	STD. ERROR
PHYS. ACTIV.	11.	495.545452	124411.274414	352.719822	106.349028
PSYCH. ACT.	11.	51.072725	937.664276	30.621304	9.232671
DOSE RATIO	11.	450.163628	71345.199219	267.105221	80.535254
STRENGTH	11.	52.849181	465.802341	21.582454	6.507355

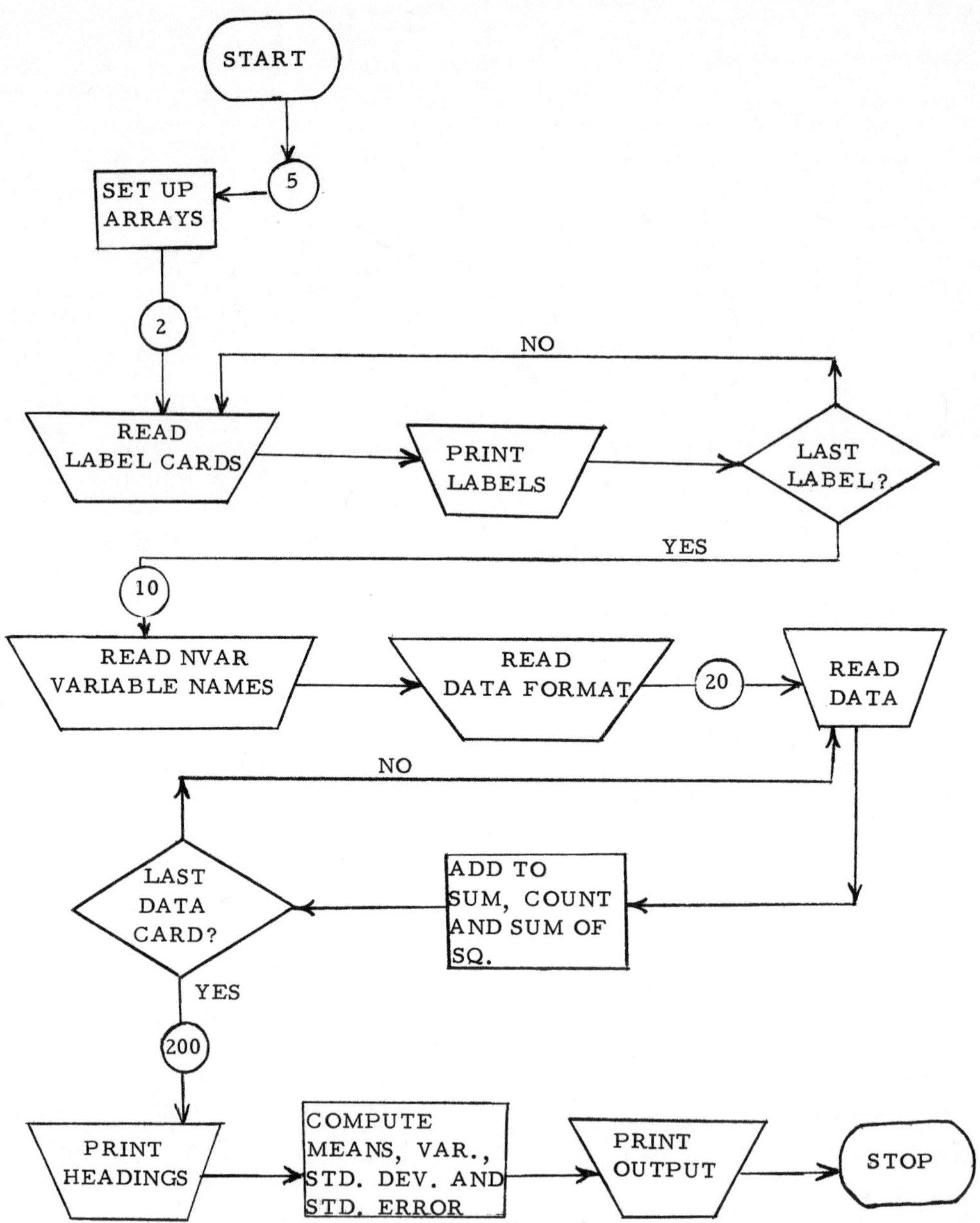
START
5
SET UP
ARRAYS
2
NO
READ
LABEL CARDS
PRINT
LABELS
LAST
LABEL?
YES
10
READ NVAR
VARIABLE NAMES
READ
DATA FORMAT
20
READ
DATA
NO
LAST
DATA
CARD?
ADD TO
SUM, COUNT
AND SUM OF
SQ.
YES
200
PRINT
HEADINGS
COMPUTE
MEANS, VAR.,
STD. DEV. AND
STD. ERROR
PRINT
OUTPUT
STOP

ABSOLUTE ADDRESS. The number permanently assigned to a particular word or character in the memory of a digital computer. This assignment is built in as part of the computer design. (Also Absolute location.)

ACCESS TIME. The time required by a digital computer to find a particular piece of information in memory and transmit it to the place where it can be used in an operation (such as the arithmetic unit).

ACCUMULATOR. A special section of memory in the arithmetic unit of a digital computer where certain operations are performed. In many digital computers all additions, subtractions, and certain logical operations take place in the accumulator.

ACCURACY. Degree of correctness or closeness to a true value. This is contrasted with precision, which is governed by the number of places. Thus, the representation of the pi as 3.14266 is more precise but less accurate than its representation as 3.142.

ADDRESS. Reference to a specific location in the memory of a digital computer.

ALGORITHM. A method of solution or calculation. The basis for a program.

ALPHAMERIC. A term referring to numbers and/or letters (a contraction of alphabetic-numeric).

ARITHMETIC UNIT. The section of a digital processor wherein computations and logical operations are performed. Thus, a computation in many computers requires the transmission of information from memory to the arithmetic unit, execution of the computational steps, and return of the computed information to memory.

ASSEMBLER. A digital computer program which operates on a source program to produce an executable machine language object program.

AUTOMATIC PROGRAMMING. A term referring to processes or techniques whereby a digital computer is used to produce programs or parts of programs without specific instructions by a human agent. Compilers, for example, make extensive use of automatic programming.

BAND. (1) See Channel. (2) A given range of frequencies.

BASE. The root on which a given number system is founded. For example, the decimal system is a base 10 system.

BATCH. A series of jobs to be run successively on a digital system without human intervention.

BCD (Binary Coded Decimal). A system for representing numbers in a digitalcomputer's memory wherein each decimal digit is represented by a binary number.

BINARY NUMBER. A number written in base-2 arithmetic (where there is no single digit higher than 1). The following chart will explain:

Decimal No.	Binary Equivalent
0	0
1	1
2	10
3	11
4	100
21	10101

BISTABLE. The property of certain systems or subsystems to operate or remain in one of only two states. A household light switch is a bistable mechanism.

BIT. The basic unit in a digital computer's logic or memory. It is bistable in that it can only assume one of two available states. These are represented as "on" or "off," "yes" or "no," and are written as 1 or 0.

BLOCK DIAGRAM. (1) A chart depicting the flow of information and logic in a particular digital computer program. (2) More generally, a schematic representation of the functional components of a given system. (Also Flowchart.)

BLOCKING. The process of running together several records of information to form one long multiple record for purposes of compact storage on magnetic tape. When block records are retrieved for subsequent use, they are deblocked into their original single record form.

BOOLIAN ALGEBRA. Named after George Boole, this system provides a mathematical basis for the manipulation of an operation with classes, sets, and various logical elements and structures. As such, it is a vital tool in computer hardware design.

BOOTSTRAP. In the context of digital computers, this is a process whereby the manual introduction of a set of very trivial instructions provide the digital processor with the ability to read in further instructions, which then add to that ability, and so on, until a complete program has been read in and stored in the processor.

BRAILLER. A program, or group of programs, which provide the blind computernik with programming, listing, and debugging aids in computer braille.

BRANCH. A decision instruction in a digital computer program which requires the processor to follow one of several alternate pathways based on the outcome of some internal comparison or other test.

BRUTE FORCE. Data-handling and analysis methods which entail the use of extensive examination and iteration techniques. These methods were generally known but not practical before the advent of computers.

BUFFER. A special section of memory in a digital computer set aside to retain information transmitted from one place until it is needed or can be accommodated by another place. A buffer may be permanently set up as part of the basic machine design or may be assigned temporarily in a given program. In the former case, for example, many digital systems are equipped with input-output buffers which allow transmission of information to and from the processor while internal processing is going on.

BYTE. A group of bits required to represent a single legitimate character of information. (Many digital processors use six bits byte, newer ones use eight.)

CALL. A reference, in a digital computer program, to another program or subprogram, which then assumes control of processing until all of its instructions have been executed, at which point it returns control to the original program.

CARD IMAGE. The representation of the information on an 80-column punched card as a single record on magnetic tape or other auxiliary storage device.

CATHODE-RAY TUBE (CRT). A peripheral device for the display of digital output as a series of reinforced signals appearing on a fluorescent screen. Many CRT units are also equipped with means for entering input.

CENTRAL PROCESSOR. See Processor.

CHANNEL. (1) An independent pathway for transmission of data to and from a processor (such as a card reader). (2) On auxiliary storage devices, such as magnetic tape, a portion of the tape parallel to the edge on which information can be stored (also known as Track or Band).

CHARACTER. Any letter, decimal digit, or special single-digit symbol (such as a punctuation symbol).

CHARACTER READER. A digital input device which is capable of recognizing printed or written characters and transmitting this information directly into a processor without prior conversion to punched cards or other computer-compatible input form (such as a magnetic check reader used by banks).

CHECK BIT. A special bit included as part of a byte in many digital processors which are designed to use a code in which any character must be represented by an odd or even number bits in the "on" status (odd or even parity). In an odd-parity machine, for example, if a particular letter is represented by an even number of bits in the "on" position, the check bit is automatically turned on to maintain odd parity. If the character happens to be represented by an odd number of bits, the check bit is automatically left off.

CLEAR. The process of erasing information contained in part or all of a digital computers memory and replacing it with some standard symbol representing blanks or zeroes.

CLOSED LOOP. A sequence of operations or events which are arranged and controlled so that the entire cycle may be automatically repeated.

CODE. (1) A short, unique representation for a given condition, magnitude, event, or observation. (2) A specific system, inherent in the design of a particular digital processor, for the internal representation of characters. (3) The process of expressing the steps in a solution of a given problem in terms which are meaningful to a computer.

COLLATING. The process of combining two or more sequences of data in such a way that the sequence of the final data file is the same as that used in the individual data components (for example, the creation of a single file from two files containing card 1 and card 2, respectively, both sequenced by patient number).

COMMAND. A specific pulse or signal transmitted to a device for the execution of a given operation.

COMPILER. A digital computer program which is written to accept a source program in some problem-oriented language and, by the use of automatic programming techniques, produce an executable object program.

COMPUTER. A device which is capable of accepting information, performing mathematical and/or logical operations on this information, and producing results of these processes. When applied to machinery, this term includes the peripheral devices required for receiving input and displaying output, as well as the central processor itself.

COMPUTER-LIMITED. The property exhibited by a program or job in which the required computation time is sufficiently long so that the input-output rate is retarded.

COMPUTERNIK. A difficult-to-define term referring to a person working with or on computers.

CONSOLE. That part of the central processor from which the computing system is operated and monitored.

CONTROL UNIT. That portion of a digital processor which interprets coded instructions and provides proper signals to the other circuits so that these instructions can be executed.

CONVERTER. A peripheral device which transfers information from one medium to another, such as a card-to-tape converter.

CORE MEMORY. A set of magnetized components which store information by assuming combinations of magnetization direction as instructed by the circuitry of the digital computer. Each individual core is a bistable magnetic element capable of storing an individual binary digit. (Also Core storage or Core.)

CYBERNETICS. The study of the operation of automatic information handling machines as compared to the communication and control components of the central nervous system.

DATA. Any information, numeric or non-numeric, coded or literal.

DATA REDUCTION. Processes for eliminating spurious data, summarizing, consolidating, and otherwise facilitating subsequent analyses and scrutiny by decreasing the volume of information. (Also see Editing.)

DEBUGGING. The processes, rituals, and incantations used by computerniks to detect and eliminate errors in their programs.

DIAGNOSTIC ROUTINE. A program or program segment built into a digital computer's operating system which is used to locate a given type of mistake in programming or input-output preparation, or an equipment malfunction.

DIGITAL COMPUTER. A device designed to process data presented to it as discrete entities.

DISK. A random-access auxiliary memory device in which information is stored on constantly rotating magnetic disks.

DOWN TIME. That time during the operating day when the computer is inoperative because of malfunctions, maintenance, or other such reasons.

DRIVE. See Tape drive.

DRUM. A random-access auxiliary memory device wherein information is stored on a revolving drum coated with magnetic material.

DUMPING. The process of transmitting part or all of the contents of a digital computer's memory to some output device.

EDITING. The process of preparing data for use in a computer or for display on an output device. A such this may include rearrangement and/or deletion. (Also see Data reduction.)

ERASE. (1) To remove coded impulses from magnetic tape, disk, etc. (2) See Clear.

EVEN PARITY. A system for representing information on some computer-compatible medium in which the code for each character is designed to contain an even number of bits in the "on" status.

EXECUTIVE PROGRAM. A set of routines which oversee the operation of a digital robot (Also Executive system, Supervisory program, etc. on automatically monitored digital robots).

EXIT. The return of control to the supervisory routines after completion of a job.

FERRITE. A composition of magnetic and oxides bound by a ceramic carrier and used for digital computer memory elements.

FIELD. A group of one or more columns in certain consecutive locations on a punched card used consistently to contain information of a certain kind.

FILE. An entire group of data pertaining to a single project or study.

FIXED POINT. A mode of expressing numbers such that the lengths (number of digits) in the integer and fraction portions conform to predetermined constant values.

FIXED WORD LENGTH. A type of digital computer in which the number of characters referred to by a single machine address is set by the processor's design.

FLOATING POINT. A means of expressing numbers in terms of coefficients and exponents of a given base number in (usually 2 or 10). Thus, the number X expressed in floating point would be $X = BN^C$

and could be written C + B with the base N implied. For example, 236 written in floating point notation using a base of 10 would be .236 + 03.

FLOWCHART. See Block diagram.

FORMAT. The general arrangement of data and identification for input and output purposes.

FORMATTING. The process of arranging input or output so that it appears in proper form when ultimately read in or displayed.

GENERAL-PURPOSE COMPUTER. A data-processing device designed to handle a variety of problems with no prior knowledge as to the nature of any of these problems.

HANGUP. The inability of a computer to continue executing instructions because of a programming error, improper input sequence, or other similar cause.

HARD COPY. Any information produced in readable form at the same time that the same information is produced on computer compatible devices.

HARDWARE. The actual equipment (electronic, electrical, and mechanical) of which computing systems are comprised.

HEAD. The recorder component used for transmission of impulses to or from a magnetic storage medium.

HIGH PUNCH. See Zone punch.

INFORMATION RETRIEVAL. A series of computer techniques for searching, recognizing, and printing data (either numbers or documents) selected from a larger file.

INPUT. Data or other information in such a form that is directly transmittible to a computer.

INPUT-OUTPUT BOUND. A job in which the actual processing time is sufficiently short that the overall rate is governed by the speed of peripheral devices.

INSTRUCTIONS. A set of legitimate machine characters which, when sensed by a digital computer, will cause a particular operation to be performed. This is not quite synonymous with the word "command" which usually implies the regeneration of an electronic signal to trigger or inhibit the action of some electrical device.

INTERPRETER. A peripheral device which will take punched cards with no printing and add the printed equivalent of the contents of the card.

INTERRECORD GAP. A length of blank tape automatically skipped by the tape drive to separate blocks.

ITERATION. A mathematical process for converging upon a result by repeated execution of a series of steps. One of the brute force techniques.

JOB. An uninterrupted processing run on a particular study or project.

KEYPUNCH. A keyboard device for recording information on punched cards.

LANGUAGE. A system of symbols and characters, each assigned a specific meaning consistent with the internal design of a computer, for use with a prescribed set of rules in communicating with a computer.

LIBRARY. An integrated collection of programs and program segments for a given computer which will handle a variety of problem solutions.

LINE PRINTER. An output device which prints an entire line of characters at a time.

LINEAR PROGRAMMING. A mathematical technique for determining the optimum value of a variable or a set of variables according to certain conditions in a system of variables whose relation to one another is linear. This technique may be programmed on a computer but is not restricted to it.

LOADER. A program segment which, when read into the memory of a digital computer, equips it for reading subsequent information.

LOADING. (1) The preparation of a reel of magnetic tape mounted on a tape drive for use by a processor. (2) Introducing instructions into a processor.

LOCATION. See Address.

LOGIC. In computers, the circuitry required for the implementation of the mathematical and manipulative operations inherent in the computer design.

LOGICAL ELEMENT. A circuit or group of circuits in a computer design to execute a particular logical function, such as an AND gate or flip-flop.

LOGICAL RECORD. All the information on one experiment, on one patient, or on one case. (A logical record could, therefore, occupy any number of physical records.)

LOGICAL UNIT. An input/output device attached to a central processor.

LOOP. (1) See Closed loop. (2) A set of instructions in a digital computer program which are repeated a prescribed number of times to achieve a desired result.

MACHINE LANGUAGE. A set of coded instructions which a digital computer can execute directly without intermediate programmed translation, conversion, or other preprocessing.

MACHINE TIME. That time during which the computer is operating.

MAGNETIC CORE. A piece of magnetic material of some given regular shape, which because of its two possible states of polarization can be used to store a binary digit of information.

MAGNETIC TAPE. Tape composed of a base such as paper, metal, or plastic coated with a magnetic material for purposes of storing information represented by polarized spots or bits.

MARK SENSE. A process whereby marks entered on a card with a special pencil can be sensed by a resistance-measuring mechanism and translated into corresponding information on punched cards.

MEGABIT. A memory unit capable of storing up to one million binary digits.

MEGABUCK. A monetary unit for measuring computer system cost.

MEMORY. Any device or assembly which can store information for subsequent extraction.

MERGING. The process of combining two or more data files sequenced in a certain manner into a single data file identically sequenced (e.g., patient records from two hospitals).

MICROPROGRAMMING. The synthesis of a mathematical or logical function from a series of very trivial elemental instructions, such as a procedure for multiplication composed of a sequence of addition instructions. Microprogramming may be a technique used by the computernik or may be a feature built into a computer's basic hardware.

MNEMONIC CODE. A code which represents a particular operation or function of a computer in a language closer to human usage.

MONITOR. (1) A device which scrutinizes a continuous event, process, or signal for purposes of observation, reporting, or control. (2) A supervisory program which regulates the processing of jobs in a digital computing system.

MULTIPROCESSING. The execution of more than one program at a time in a given computer. A computer capable of multiprocessing must, therefore, be equipped with more than one set of arithmetic and control units.

NANOSECOND. A billionth of a second.

NOISE. Any electrical signal or disturbance which distorts or otherwise interferes with a desired signal being transmitted on the same device.

NORMALIZATION. Adjustment of a signal, variable, or other piece of information to some standard or reference value.

OBJECT PROGRAM. A set of sequential instructions in direct machine language. Usually produced from a source program using a compiler.

OCTAL NUMBER. A number written in base-8 arithmetic (where there is no single digit higher than 7). The chart below gives examples:

Decimal No.	Octal Equivalent
0	0
1	1
7	7
8	10
16	20
100	144

ODD PARITY. A system for representing information on some computer-compatible medium in which the code for each character is designed to contain an odd number of bits in the "on" status.

OFFLINE. A setup in which the components of a computing system or the input mechanism and the computer are not directly linked and cannot communicate electronically.

ONLINE. A method of operation in which the data-generating or display mechanism is electronically connected to the processor.

OPERATING SYSTEM. In digital computers, a complex of supervisory programs which include assemblers, compilers, monitors, and other executive components.

OUTPUT. Results produced by a computing system and transmitted to some peripheral device.

OVERFLOW. A condition where a computed result is produced whose magnitude is beyond the range of the component which must accomodate it. In analog computers this would be a voltage beyond the operating range; in digital processors this might be a number too large for the counter in which it is to appear.

OVERPUNCH. See Zone punch.

PATTERN RECOGNITION. Digital programming techniques for defining and comparing repeatable sequences of characters in data files.

PERFORATED TAPE. Paper tape in which information is represented by a series of punched holes (also Punched tape).

PERIPHERAL DEVICE. An electronic information-handling unit other than a central processor. In this context, on- and offline units are considered peripheral devices.

PHYSICAL RECORD. A single card or card image.

PLOTTER. An output device on which can be displayed a graph of one variable against one or more others.

PRECISION. The number of significant digits attached to a value.

PROGRAM. A series of sequential instructions, coded in computer-compatible language for the performance of some processing task (also used to name the process of preparing programs).

PROGRAM SYSTEM. See Operating system.

PUNCHED CARD. A card of standard dimensions containing a fixed number of places where holes representing coded information can be punched.

RANDOM ACCESS. Access to a location in storage which is in no way dependent on the previous location accessed.

RANDOM NUMBER. A number constructed of digits which are obtained by a process in which any given digit is just as likely to appear next as any other digit.

READING. The process by which information is transmitted from a peripheral device to a processor.

READOUT. An online apparatus which produces readable observations of data as they are generated.

REAL TIME. A computational setup in which the time-varying parameter is generated at its actual rate.

REGISTER. A special section in a digital processor for the temporary storage of information.

REPRODUCE HEAD. The component in a magnetic storage device which senses magnetic impulses on the storage medium, producing corresponding signals.

REPRODUCTION. (1) The duplication of a data file, signal, or other information. (2) Display of a previously recorded signal. (Also Playback.)

RESET. The return of a register or other processor component to a zero or initial condition.

REWIND. To reset a reel of magnetic tape to its starting point.

ROBOT. A multi-component system which may or may not include human beings, capable of responding in a consistent and logical manner to a wide variety of input signals, producing required output.

ROBOTICS. The techniques, disciplines, and attitudes involved in designing, developing, and working with robots.

ROUTINE. A program or program segment designed for the execution of a given mathematical function or cohesive operation.

RUN. A single execution of a program on a processor.

SCALING. The process of changing the range of a set of variables in a given problem so that the problem may be accommodated on a given computer.

SCANNER. A decision-making component which reads and examines a sampled or entire data file, instigating appropriate action if certain criteria are or are not met.

SCREENING. Systematic examination of a data file and subsequent division of that file into a number of subfiles based on certain prescribed criteria. The simplest type of screen would produce two subfiles ("interesting" and "uninteresting").

SENSE SWITCH. One of a series of switches on the console of the digital computer which allows the operator to control certain portions of a program externally. The status of each sense switch (on or off) can be tested in the program and appropriate action prescribed.

SIGNIFICANT DIGITS. The number of digits appearing in a piece of information when that information is written as a number between 1 and 10 times a base raised to a power. As such, it is a reflection of the precision associated with that piece of information. Thus, for example, the numbers of 12,000 and 12,000,000 both contain the same number of significant digits (two).

SIMULATION. The representation of the behavior of a physical system on some other system intended to imitate that behavior.

SOFTWARE. Programs, routines and other logical structures which enable the computer hardware to perform.

SORTER. A peripheral machine which segregates cards according to the location of the holes punched in a given column. Sorting may also be performed with a processor using information on magnetic tape or other mediums.

SOURCE PROGRAM. A set of sequential instructions written in language fairly close to the vernacular (i.e., symbols and instruction codes are close to their corresponding names). The computer is not able to store or carry out such instructions, and conversion to an object program via a compiler or assembler is necessary.

SPECIAL-PURPOSE COMPUTER. A computer in which a processing program is built into the basic machine design (e.g., many aircraft or missile computers).

STORAGE. See Memory.

SUBPROGRAM. A program segment, used in a larger main program, which is designed to produce a certain function or operation. (See Routine.)

SUBROUTINE. A pretested program segment for performing some mathematical or logical task. Once it is included in a program, a subroutine may be referenced any number of times in various sections of the program without having to store duplicate instructions. (Also Subprogram.)

SUPERVISORY PROGRAM. See Executive program.

TAPE DRIVE. A magnetic tape transport for recording and playback of data.

TIME-SHARING. The technique of providing access for several users to a single digital processor by allocating consecutive small increments of the total available time to each user in rotation or on a priority basis.

TRACK. See Channel.

UPDATING. The process of incorporating recent information in its proper place in a data file. When working with digital data on magnetic tape, for example, an updating program examines new information, compares it with the information already recorded on the current data tape, modifies the record where appropriate, and creates a new data tape which incorporates all the changes.

UPTIME. That time during the day when the computing system is doing productive work or is available for such work. (Same as Down time but upside down.)

VARIABLE WORD LENGTH. A type of digital computer in which the number of characters which constitutes one machine word is not fixed and is under the control of the programmer.

VERIFIER. A machine similar to the keypunch which is used to compare the data on punched cards with those on the collection sheets.

WORD. The smallest logical unit in a computer's memory to which a location can be assigned.

WRITING. The process of transmitting output to a peripheral device.

ZONE PUNCH. A hole punched in any of the three top rows of a standard punched card.

INDEX